Praise for Tuning You...

"*Tuning Your Heart to Worship* speaks to my heart with reassuring insights. With each day's entry, Dr. Lavon Gray will lead you on an intimate journey into the psalms, where you will find your heart longing for more of those moments that can only be found in the presence of God."

—Babbie Mason, Dove Award–winning singer-songwriter, author, and television talk show host

"This wonderful resource, centered on my 'favorite' book of the Bible, is devotional in nature and highly practical in format. Using real-world experience and anecdotes, along with solid scriptural principles, Dr. Gray helps modern day believers apply God's Word to daily issues. It is refreshing and genuine. This book will become one of your favorites!"

—Dr. Frank S. Page, president and chief executive officer, Executive Committee of the Southern Baptist Convention

"I have been friends with Dr. Lavon Gray for many years. I have always been inspired by his love for the church and his leadership in worship ministry. *Tuning Your Heart to Worship* is a wonderful journey through the Book of Psalms. I am so excited for the rest of the world to have the opportunity to experience this take on the book of songs and have the psalms come to life in a whole new way. Love this book!"

—Mark Harris, associate senior pastor, worship, Gateway Church, Dallas, TX

"No one understands musicians like another musician, which is why I so enjoyed Dr. Lavon Gray's insights on the psalms. His lifelong love for the Hebrew Hymnbook—the Book of Psalms—has given us a rich set of readable truths that tune our hearts to worship and make our souls sing. Lavon takes us through the symphony of the psalms with great stories and practical insights for each day. *Tuning Your Heart to Worship* will help turn your eyes to Jesus."

—Robert J. Morgan, pastor, author, and speaker

"This collection of daily devotions is incredible, inspirational, and full of practical application crafted from the Book of Psalms with a touch of humor, insightful application to real-life experiences, and solid biblical interpretation. Lavon has created a practical, warm, engaging, and encouraging handbook that should help all of us focus more on our Lord and less on our changing circumstances. This is a must-read for all students of the psalms and worshippers of Jehovah."

—Vernon M. Whaley, PhD, dean, School of Music, Liberty University

"Dr. Lavon Gray's depth of insight into Scripture is wonderful and encourages me to probe daily, deeper and deeper, into worship and the Word. Thank you, Dr. Gray!"

—Dr. Leo Day, dean and professor of voice, School of Church Music,
Southwestern Baptist Theological Seminary

"Spending time with Lavon Gray has been a life enriching experience for me as a local church worship pastor. He not only loves God but his love for church worship is contagious. *Tuning Your Heart to Worship* is a daily guide to help us enter into a fresh daily experience with God. Lavon has captured the essence of worship through the Book of Psalms, and this book will be a source of encouragement to all who read it."

—Ray Jones, worship pastor, Community Bible Church,
San Antonio, TX

"The Book of Psalms has been a powerful encouragement to countless souls for thousands of years. Now, Dr. Lavon Gray sheds new light on these ancient masterpieces of praise by delivering fresh and insightful devotions that are not only fun to read but practical in application. I highly recommend this book. You will be encouraged and blessed, and it will deepen your walk as a worshipper of the one true God."

—Charles Billingsley, worship leader,
Shadow Mountain Community Church, San Diego, CA

"Life can be a roller coaster. In *Tuning Your Heart to Worship*, Dr. Lavon Gray offers a practical and biblical perspective of the child of God navigating the ups and downs of life by walking through the psalms. Lament, joy, heartbreak, and praise—it's all here. This book should be on the nightstands of fellow travelers."

—Mike Harland, director, LifeWay Worship Resources

"From the pen of Lavon Gray, a man who lives what he believes, comes a convincing, convicting, and contagious devotional. The only people who won't like this devotional are the ones who haven't read it yet."

—Derric Johnson, pastor and author, musician and
creative consultant, Walt Disney World (retired)

"*Tuning Your Heart to Worship* is a 100-day journey through the psalms every worship leader and worshipper should take. Thank you, Dr. Gray, for being our guide on such an amazing journey."

—Dr. Roger Breland, executive director, University of Mobile Center for
Performing Arts, and member, Gospel Music Hall of Fame

"Dr. Lavon Gray's *Tuning Your Heart to Worship* does just that—tunes your heart to worship. With a mixture of story, Scripture interpretation, pathos, and humor, this devotional guide will enrich both your personal and corporate worship. Use it for 100 days—then start over again!"

> —Dr. David W. Music, professor of church music, Baylor University

"*Tuning Your Heart to Worship* is more than a ministry resource; it is a refuge. It will take permanent residence on my study desk as a valued source of inspiration and insight. I will use it personally and will share its insights to influence worship leaders and musicians within my ministry."

> —Dr. D. Doran Bugg, minister of music and worship,
> First Baptist Church, Dallas, TX

"There is nothing better than reading and obeying God's Word. Thank you, Dr. Gray, for this practical book. I will use it, and I encourage others to do the same."

> —Scott C. White, senior minister of music and worship,
> First Baptist Church Woodstock, Woodstock, GA

"If you love a great story, and if you thrill before a grand anthem, then Dr. Lavon Gray's book *Tuning Your Heart to Worship* will quickly become one of your favorites. This worship leader extraordinaire has opened the Book of Psalms to show us more of its riches, and in doing so, he prods us to a stronger obedience and deeper faithfulness."

> —Dr. Joe McKeever, pastor, author, and cartoonist

"In *Tuning Your Heart to Worship*, Dr. Lavon Gray reminds us that our private worship lays the foundation for our public worship. So instead of depending on our own contrived language, he points to a text that has already been prepared for us in the Book of Psalms. If you ponder and live with these daily devotions, they will provide a rich worship foundation for 100 days and beyond."

> —Dr. David Manner—associate executive director,
> Kansas-Nebraska Convention of Southern Baptists

"*Tuning Your Heart to Worship* is a must-read for those who are searching for biblically based inspiration and motivation. Using the Book of Psalms as textual basis, Dr. Lavon Gray weaves inspirational stories and helps the reader navigate the waters of life. It is something that needs to be by the bedside—to read before going to sleep and there when we awaken from rest. This book will make your heart sing!"

> —Dr. C. David Keith, dean, Townsend School of Music,
> Mercer University

"My favorite thing about the Book of Psalms is that there is a chapter and moment for every road we will walk in this life. When we face ups, downs, hardships, happiness, enemies, defeat, grief, times of worship, or anything else, there is a psalm for that. The words and truths of these passages are just as life giving today as they have ever been. Dr. Gray gives such a fresh and relevant look at each of these psalms. He beautifully connects each truth with our lives and practically teaches how we can connect, learn, grow, and apply them throughout our day. I encourage everyone who has the heart of a worshipper to partake of this tremendous resource."

—John Bolin, minister of worship and arts,
Houston's First Baptist Church, Houston, TX

"An informed worshipper understands the absolute necessity of regular meditation on the psalms. This is God's treasure book for worship pastors today, timeless and ever so generous in its multiplicity of applications for daily living! You can't get enough of it. As God inspired David to write eternal truths, so I believe God has worked in Lavon's heart to bless us with fresh inspiration, wonderfully crafted in bite-sized, poignant moments to assist us in personal worship. Lavon is a gifted writer and communicator, a worship pastor and friend whose ministry is driven by God's Word. This new devotional book will find its place at the top of my stack of daily Bible studies!"

—Slater Murphy, director of church music,
Mississippi Baptist Convention Board

"Lavon Gray has blessed us with a set of 100 thought-filled devotions on select psalms that lead us not only to reflect on God's Word but also to encounter the Lord Himself. Sprinkled with personal stories and illustrations from Scripture and historical figures and events, Dr. Gray challenges the reader to linger in God's presence and then to meditate, pray, journal, and apply the truth about God found in each psalm. Written from the perspective of a pastor and church musician, *Tuning Your Heart to Worship* is a spiritual refueling station that guides the reader to 'delight in God' and to 'pursue Him all the days of my life.'"

—J. Stanley Moore, DMA, senior fellow and professor of church music
and worship, B. H. Carroll Theological Institute

Tuning Your Heart to

WORSHIP

*A Worshipper's Journey
through the Psalms Devotional*

L. LAVON GRAY

Birmingham, Alabama

New Hope® Publishers
PO Box 12065
Birmingham, AL 35202-2065
NewHopePublishers.com
New Hope Publishers is a division of WMU®.

Library of Congress Cataloging-in-Publication Data

Names: Gray, L. Lavon, 1967- author.
Title: Tuning your heart to worship : a worshipper's journey through the
 Psalms devotional / L. Lavon Gray.
Description: First [edition]. | Birmingham : New Hope Publishers, 2017.
Identifiers: LCCN 2017033656 | ISBN 9781625915320 (permabind)
Subjects: LCSH: Bible. Psalms—Devotional literature.
Classification: LCC BS1430.54 .G73 2017 | DDC 223/.207—dc23
LC record available at https://lccn.loc.gov/2017033656

ISBN-13: 978-1-62591-532-0
N184106 • 1017 • 1.5M1

This book is dedicated to godly worshippers
who shaped my life growing up and in each of
the churches I've been honored to serve:

Everett Baptist Church, Mendenhall, Mississippi

Main Street Baptist Church, Mendenhall, Mississippi

County Line Baptist Church, Mendenhall, Mississippi

D'Lo Baptist Church, D'Lo, Mississippi

West Union Baptist Church, Carriere, Mississippi

First Baptist Church, Wiggins, Mississippi

Haltom Road Baptist Church, Fort Worth, Texas

First Baptist Church, McComb, Mississippi

First Baptist Church, Taylors, South Carolina

First Baptist Church, Jackson, Mississippi

Contents

A Word from Lavon

*The most valuable thing the Psalms do for me is to express
the same delight in God which made David dance.*
                                    —C. S. Lewis

I 've started my mornings the same way for more than ten years:
reading five psalms a day. In addition to immersing myself into
the actual songbook of Jesus (yes, He actually sang the psalms),
this approach allows me to meditate on all 150 psalms every month.
Each morning I'm able to experience God working in the lives of His
people. The fall of man in Eden? It's in the psalms. God's covenant
with Abraham? Yes. Moses and the burning bush, the parting of the
Red Sea, and the receiving of the Law on Mount Sinai? Absolutely.
In fact, it's all in there . . . the entire Old Testament story of God
working through His people—from creation through the return from
Babylonian exile—is at our fingertips. The psalms have an important
historical function: they help us relive the work of God in His people.

Just as important, the psalms explore every emotional aspect of
our Christian walk. From the high praise of Psalm 100 when the
psalmist declares, "Shout triumphantly to the LORD, all the earth"
(v. 1) to the dark despair of Psalm 119, "I am weary from grief" (v. 28)
they penetrate our spirits deeper than any book of the Bible. Simply
stated, the psalms mirror life.

There are several things I want to mention as we begin our journey
as worshippers through this amazing book of the Bible. First, this
is not an academic study of the psalter. There are many commentar-
ies and scholarly resources available to help Christians explore the
structure, historical context, and theological content of each psalm.
While I recommend researching all those elements for a deeper
understanding of the psalms, our approach is more practical. With
this in mind, here are five keys to help you over the next 100 days:

> **Journal:** In addition to this book, you will need your Bible
> and a journal. Reading supporting Scripture, as well as
> writing down key thoughts and insights, is critical in study-
> ing the psalms.

Read the entire psalm: Although the devotions usually focus on one to three key verses, take time to read the entire psalm. I'm positive the Lord will bring other themes to your mind that will apply to your life. Write them down so you will remember.

Read the devotional: You should be able to read each devotional in a few, short minutes, but don't rush. Allow the content to penetrate your mind. All 100 devotionals are centered on one central idea. Make sure you identify this theme as you read the devotional and journal your responses.

Pray: Each day there is a suggested prayer to help guide your time with the Lord. These are my personal prayers I prayed when writing each devotional. These written prayers are only a starting point. Pour out your heart to God in an honest response to His revelation.

What Next? Each devotional concludes with practical suggestions for application. Don't skip this section. This is where the psalms take root in your life.

Acknowledgments

This journey would not have been possible without Judy Patterson and the excellent team at New Hope Publishers. Ramona Richards, managing editor, and the entire editorial team provided excellent support throughout the entire process.

Cille Litchfield, who proofreads every word I write, is actually more like a sister than a friend. This is our fourth book project together, and I'm enormously grateful for her partnership in these writing endeavors. My administrative assistant, Terry Sims, painstakingly manages my schedule and helps me balance deadlines and ministry requirements. Our entire worship staff at First Jackson, including Eva Hart, Tim Walker, Nick Hardeman, and James Arrington Goff, makes such a contribution to my life and ministry that a book like this would not be possible without them.

My wife of almost three decades, Wendy, is the most amazing woman I've ever met. Since our first walk on the beach in August 1987, she has made me a better person and a more effective worship pastor. My older daughters and my sons-in-law, Kayla (Chris) and Lizzie (Tyler) model the passion for Jesus that defines so many Christian Millennials. I'm thankful for all they've taught me on my journey as a worshipper. Also, my youngest daughter, Katibeth, who still lives at home, has sacrificed a lot of dad time so I could complete this project. I'm sure payback will involve a visit to Orlando very soon.

Finally, to the thousands of worshippers across the world who I've had the privilege to lead to the throne of God, thank you for an amazing journey. And just think . . . it only gets better from here!

> *Then I looked and heard the voice of many angels around the throne, and also of the living creatures and of the elders. Their number was countless thousands, plus thousands of thousands. They said with a loud voice: The Lamb who was slaughtered is worthy to receive power and riches and wisdom and strength and honor and glory and blessing! I heard every creature in heaven, on earth, under*

the earth, on the sea, and everything in them say: Blessing and honor and glory and dominion to the One seated on the throne, and to the Lamb, forever and ever!

—Revelation 5:11–13

Tuning Your Heart to
WORSHIP

Day 1

Which Path Will You Take?

How happy is the man who does not follow the advice of the wicked or take the path of sinners or join a group of mockers! Instead, his delight is in the LORD's instruction, and he meditates on it day and night.

—*Psalm 1:1-2*

One of my favorite memories from growing up in rural Mississippi is of late night "coon hunts" with my grandfather. The excitement of those nights spent crawling through ravines, wading across creeks, and swimming through thickets of undisturbed undergrowth is as real today as it was more than four decades ago.

Although I didn't learn a lot about hunting during those moonlit adventures (in fact, I never remember seeing a raccoon, much less catching one), my grandfather used these times to teach an important lesson about navigating the woods: make sure you stay on the *right* path. You see, the woods are filled with all sorts of paths. My grandfather walked the safe ones night after night, week after week, and year after year. That's why we never found ourselves lost in the dark of the woods—never. We stayed on the *right* path.

As our journey begins, the psalmist sets two distinct paths before us: one defined by happiness, the other by ruin. Just as my grandfather pointed us to the right path through the woods, the psalmist provides clear instructions for navigating the journey of life: delight in the Lord's instruction, and meditate on it day and night.

This first psalm, an introduction to the rest of the book, vividly contrasts two approaches to life. Blessings await those who delight in God's Word, while hopelessness and misery characterize the life of the wicked. Two paths . . . two destinations . . . the journey determined by the impact of God's Word in your life. If seeking a lifestyle of worship, His Word must become central to all we do.

Which path will you choose? One is filled with laughter and joy, the other with regret and sorrow. The choice is yours.

All Scripture is inspired by God and is profitable for teaching, for rebuking, for correcting, for training in righteousness, so that the man of God may be complete, equipped for every good work.

—2 Timothy 3:16–17

prayer

Father in heaven, forgive me for not meditating on Your Word and not allowing it to permeate every fiber of my being. Today I pray I will allow Your instruction to guide every aspect of my life and that the joy of walking with You will be clear to those around me. In the name of Jesus Christ, Your Son, I pray. Amen.

What Next?

What role does the Word of God play in your life? Do you delight in the instruction of the Lord? Have you prioritized time in your schedule to meditate on what He is teaching you? If so, what is He teaching you? If not, why not?

Make a commitment today to meditate on Psalm 1 and seek God's instruction for your life. It will change everything about your day!

Day 2

Is There Any Hope?

Lord, how my foes increase! There are many who attack me. Many say about me, "There is no help for him in God." But You, Lord, are a shield around me, my glory, and the One who lifts up my head.

—Psalm 3:1–3

Do you ever feel the world is out to get you?

Henry Ford's first two car companies failed before he founded Ford Motor Company. Lucille Ball failed early in her acting career, unable to land anything but B movie roles. Soichiro Honda was turned down for a job with Toyota before starting his own company. Bill Gates dropped out of Harvard and experienced a business failure before starting Microsoft. Walt Disney was fired as a newspaperman for a "lack of imagination." The rest, as they say, is history.

Sometimes life simply doesn't work out the way we've planned. Things seem to smoothly move along then, *BAM*, out of nowhere, we're knocked off our feet. In that instant, everything changes. These life-altering gut punches take on many forms . . . divorce, bankruptcy, infertility, cancer . . . but their common denominator is they can shake us and leave us feeling as though all hope is lost.

Such was the case with David. The great king, loved by all Israel, faced the unimaginable: his son, Absalom, betrayed him and organized a coup against him (2 Samuel 15–19). Not only did David face a threat against his throne, but he faced the reality that his son had not simply turned *from* him but *against* him.

In this time of intense pain, fear, and sorrow, David embraced the only One who can sustain him: "You, Lord, are a shield around me, my glory, and the One who lifts up my head." When faced with seemingly hopeless situations, how will we respond? Will it be with desperation? Anger? Fear? Or will we respond like David?

Remember, no matter what you're facing, our God stands with you and brings hope when all seems lost.

prayer

Lord, I confess that when unexpected things come my way, they may cause my faith to falter. Help me focus on the truth that You are my shield and defender in the midst of chaos. Thank You for Your unfailing love that sustains me in times of fear. Help me respond with a spirit of hope. In Jesus' name. Amen.

What Next?

Make a list of unexpected circumstances you've faced.

What emotions did you experience?

How did you respond?

What was the eventual outcome?

Read Psalm 3 and pray, asking God to work in specific areas of your life. Record your prayer in a journal.

Day 3

Sleep, Blessed Sleep

You have put more joy in my heart than they have when their grain and new wine abound. I will both lie down and sleep in peace, for You alone, LORD, make me live in safety.

—Psalm 4:7–8

E rnest Hemingway, the famed American author, once quipped, "I love sleep. My life has the tendency to fall apart when I'm awake." Unfortunately, it's the falling apart that too many times keeps us awake. We lie in bed, groggily glancing at the clock every hour, as our mind races through a checklist of problems: family, relationships, money, work. You know the drill . . . life in general.

Although we spend about one-third of our life doing it, research tells us roughly one-in-three Americans suffer from sleep deprivation. Aside from the potential health risks, the impact on our mental health is enormous. When we are stressed, we often don't sleep because our minds are cluttered with the falling apart times of life. When we don't sleep, our mental focus is weaker and our ability to clearly navigate life is greatly diminished. Sleep is a much-needed friend.

Psalm 4 finds David in distress. His honor has been insulted, and he is angry. In the center of chaos, however, he focuses on the joy the Lord has placed in his heart and the safety that comes from his presence. In the midst of the challenges of life he finds peace. This particular song is to be accompanied by strings. It's no coincidence that a psalm dealing with peace would use the most soothing of musical instruments to help deliver its message.

Several years ago, my life was in overdrive. Nothing was normal. Sick parents, teenage girls, and church issues had contributed to my lack of sleep. When I did manage to doze off, it only lasted three to four hours. After a few months of this, I was exhausted physically, mentally, and spiritually. The area most impacted, however, was my worship. I was unable, or unwilling, to spend time with God. In my weariness I had disconnected from the one source that could give me peace. Everyone around me paid a price for my weariness, but I suffered most. It was only when I, like David, focused on the joy that God had placed in my life that peace was restored to my life.

Is your life in disarray to the point that sleep is elusive? If so, take time today to focus on the joy that comes through Jesus Christ. When we do this, troubles tend to fade and hope rises to define our way forward.

prayer

Oh Great Comforter, I ask for Your peace to fill my life today. Because we live in a world gone crazy, please allow Your arms of protection to embrace me. Allow me to live in You today and the reality of Your hand of protection bring peace to my life. Amen.

What Next?

Read Psalm 4 and highlight sources of distress in David's life.

Take a few minutes to list five things that keep you awake at night.

How many are under your direct control? How many are beyond your influence?

In your own words, write a short prayer asking for peace in your life today.

Day 4

Is Your Life in Tune?

At daybreak, LORD, You hear my voice; at daybreak I plead my case to You and watch expectantly.

—Psalm 5:3

If you've ever attended a symphony concert, then you've heard it. Just before time to begin, the oboist plays a single note for the rest of the orchestra to tune their instruments to—an A=440 Hertz to be precise. For the next 60 seconds or so, the other instruments join in playing random notes and rhythmic patterns. While this cacophony of sound appears to be a hot musical mess, the preconcert tuning is indispensable. Without it, the musicians have no musical point of reference. J. Hudson Taylor, who served as a missionary to China for 51 years, understood this when he said, "Do not have your concert first, and tune your instruments afterward. Begin the day with the Word of God and prayer, and get first of all into harmony with Him."

How much time do you spend tuning your life for the challenges of the day? It's really simple: when we begin our day by tuning our heart *to* His, the rest of the day is lived in harmony *with* Him. This daily tuning session is not optional for those desiring a closer walk with the Lord. It is a way of life.

The African-American spiritual was born in the cotton fields of pre–Civil War America. While rising in response to the brutal institution of slavery, this genre of music gave voice to hope in the midst of pain and suffering. One such spiritual, "Give Me Jesus," enjoys widespread popularity today because of recordings by Fernando Ortega and others. This simple yet powerful song embodies the theme of Psalm 5:3:

🎶

In the morning when I rise,
In the morning when I rise,
In the morning when I rise,
Give me Jesus.

🎵

When we begin our day begging for Jesus, our lives and our worship are forever changed. Pretense is replaced by authenticity. Arrogance with brokenness. Ritualism with newness.

Through the death and Resurrection of Jesus, we are reconciled to Him, taking on His attributes and becoming like Him. The Apostle Paul reminded us of this when he said, "Therefore, if anyone is in Christ, he is a new creation; old things have passed away, and look, new things have come" (2 Corinthians 5:17).

Becoming like Jesus. Now that's the way to start your day!

prayer

Father, I confess that many times my life is out of tune with Yours. Help me make my time with You a priority so my worship will be fresh and meaningful. Protect my time with You each day. Help me to expectantly observe as your will is fulfilled throughout the day. Amen.

What Next?

How in tune with God is your life? What are things you can do to make your time with God more impactful?

Take five minutes to write a prayer asking God to help you hear His voice. Pray this prayer at least three times today.

Day 5

Are You Broken?

I am weary from my groaning; with my tears I dampen
my pillow and drench my bed every night. My eyes are
swollen from grief; they grow old because of all my enemies.
—Psalm 6:6–7

Several years ago while out of town on business, I made my nightly phone call to check in on the home front. To my dismay, Wendy (my wife) answered the phone crying uncontrollably. To make matters worse, I could hear my daughters wailing in the background. After what seemed like an eternity of sobbing, the girls explained they had just watched *My Dog Skip,* an autobiographical movie based on the novel of the same name by award-winning author Willie Morris. If you've never seen the movie, it traces the childhood friendship between Morris and his dog Skip, a spunky little terrier, while growing up in rural Mississippi. As in all great dog movies (spoiler alert), Skip dies, sending my family into a spiral of emotional despair. After a few minutes of long-distance counseling, eventually everyone settled down and moved on to a happier conversation. By the way, I called back the next afternoon to the same emotional minefield . . . they had watched the movie again!

Truth is, many things can make us cry—things like a bad grade, a physical injury, an argument with a friend, divorce, the death of a family member. Some of these circumstances may even break us. But how long has it been since you were broken before the Lord? I mean *really* broken.

In Psalm 6, David is completely and utterly broken. He writes that his eyes are "swollen from grief" and uses words like *weak, shaking, terror,* and *weary.* He is an emotional wreck but not because of some event or something that had been done by another person. No, David is broken because of his own sin . . . his own failures . . . his own actions.

As worshippers, we come before the Lord far too many times with a sense of pride and entitlement, ignoring the sinful state of our lives. We act like we have the right to enter His presence. In reality, nothing we do, no skill set or credential we achieve, gives us the right to worship God. Only His grace on our lives, through the blood of Jesus, allows us access to His throne. When we understand this truth, the layers of arrogance and pride that define us melt away like snow in the spring sunlight.

When we see Him for who He is, brokenness comes naturally.

prayer

God of heaven, thank You for the privilege of coming into Your presence. I confess that at times my sinful nature is masked by my own pride and arrogance. Allow me to look onto Your holiness and to sense Your presence so that my own unworthiness can be exposed. Break my spirit, Lord, so that Your character defines me. Thank You for hearing my plea for forgiveness and for allowing me access to You through Your Son, Jesus Christ. Amen.

What Next?

How many times have you been genuinely broken before the Lord?

As a worshipper, are you defined by humbleness and brokenness or arrogance and pride?

Make a list of unconfessed sin in your life, and ask God to remove them from your life.

Day 6

Under Attack!

*Yahweh my God, I seek refuge in You; save me from all
my pursuers and rescue me or they will tear me like a lion,
ripping me apart with no one to rescue me.*

—Psalm 7:1-2

W hat comes to mind when you think of David? A shepherd
boy victorious over a giant? A king specifically chosen
by God? A man after God's own heart? An extravagant
worshipper before the Lord? A warrior victorious in battle?

While all of these are true, David's life was marked by conflict,
struggle, and opposition, including his childhood battle with Goliath, King Saul's hatred and pursuit of him, and even rebellion from
his own son, Absalom. Once David assumed the throne, he faced
both external attacks from surrounding nations and internal attacks,
even from within his own family, to overthrow him. Even though
David was anointed by God and is described as a "man after God's
own heart" (1 Samuel 13:14), he faced intense opposition throughout
his life.

Today, all across the globe, thousands of Christians are being
persecuted for their faith in Jesus Christ. In 2016 alone, more than
90,000 Christians were killed because of their faith, about one
every six minutes. Though not with the intensity or violence levels
of international persecution, Christians in the United States are
facing growing levels of persecution.

While attending an art exhibit in the early 1950s, Japanese
author Shusaku Endo encountered an item that drastically impacted
his life. The item, called a *fumie*, was a simple wooden box with a
bronze engraving of Christ on the Cross. It was created in the seven-
teenth century during a period of severe persecution of Christians
in Japan. What truly captured Endo's attention, however, was that
the image of Christ had been rubbed smooth and the black foot-
prints that stained the box from the hundreds of peasants given a

choice: trample it and renounce their faith or face torture and death. Endo, a Christian since the age of 11 or 12, reportedly asked himself, "Would I too have trampled on that image?"

When attacked for your faith, how will you respond? Will you, like David, seek refuge in God, or will we trample on the very faith we claim?

prayer

Oh God, our Refuge in time of desperation, draw me close to You. Allow me to see that times of conflict and opposition are opportunities to grow in my relationship with You. Place Your arms around those believers being persecuted around the world, and give me the courage to never trample the faith that is mine through Your precious Son. Amen.

What Next?

Take a few minutes to define in your own words what it means for God to be our refuge. Make a list of ways you trample on your faith each day, and commit to stand firm in the midst of opposition.

Day 7

Worship from Chaos

What is man that You remember him, the son of man that You look after him? You made him little less than God and crowned him with glory and honor.

—Psalm 8:4–5

O ne of my choir members joined the choir on a Wednesday night after hearing the worship choir of First Baptist Church of Jackson, Mississippi, sing Tom Fettke's "The Majesty and Glory of Your Name." She is convinced that when she enters heaven's gates, this anthem will float on the air as the heavenly hosts welcome her. I can't say I disagree. This psalm is worship—it doesn't define worship—it *is* worship.

In Psalm 8:4–5, the psalmist acknowledges the Son of God— Jesus. God allowed Jesus to suffer in the most horrible ways yet God glorified Him. And He did it for me.

During the funeral of a former choir member and the wife of our minister of music emeritus, our choir sang this anthem. Our church loves this anthem. Our choir doesn't just sing it, they experience it. They worship!

♫

Alleluia! Alleluia!
The majesty and glory of Your name.

♫

The climax builds from here. However, during the funeral, something awful happened. Our massive organ suffered what was later diagnosed as a grand cypher. It was grand all right, coming from the chambers behind the choir and filling the worship center. The air was sucked out of that massive room. Several talked about how satanic it seemed—the devil just doing his best to stop our worship. Yet, the husband of the deceased, one of the most gracious men of

30

God I have ever known, stepped up, gave everyone time to regroup, and asked us to sing it again. In his mind, this was not going to rob his worship—our worship.

My heart always stirs when I hear this anthem. I think about how, like David, I have observed the exorbitance of creation from my deck at night, from the sea, the mountains, and the desert as I have traveled the world, in my own private worship times, and in the eyes of this hurting husband and father who comforted others in his time of loss and brought us back to worship from the brink of chaos.

𝄻

Alleluia! Alleluia!
The majesty and glory of Your name.

♫

prayer

Lord, You are the Lord my Lord. Thank You for Your Son Jesus. I praise You. I love You. I thank You for being the creator and author of all things good and never the creator of chaos. Amen.

What Next?

Meditate on Psalm 8.

List times in your life where God provided something or someone through chaos to help bring your focus back to Him.

Day 8

It's All in a Name

Those who know Your name trust in You because You have not abandoned those who seek You, Yahweh.

—Psalm 9:10

Names are important. When our girls were born we spent much time selecting just the right names: Kayla, Lizzie, and Katibeth. Now those names are inseparable from their personalities. In a sense, their names help us define who they are.

In biblical times, a person's name was often connected to their character or mission in life.

Adam named his wife Eve, which means life, because she was mother of all the living (Genesis 3:20). God changed Abram's name to Abraham, which means "father of many nations" (Genesis 17:5). God changed Sarai's name to Sarah, which means "princess" (Genesis 17:15). He changed Jacob's name to Israel, a word in Hebrew that sounds like "he struggled with God" (Genesis 32:28). And when Gabriel appeared to Mary, she was told "you are to name Him Jesus, because He will save His people from their sins" (Matthew 1:21).

Psalm 9 reminds us that knowing God's name allows us to place unfaltering trust in Him. Here are some of the most common:

Abba: Father

Adonai: LORD, Master

Alpha and Omega: Beginning and End

Attiyq Youm: The Ancient of Days

Christos: The Anointed One

El Chuwl: The God Who Gave You Birth

El Deah: God of Knowledge

El Elyon: The God Most High

El Olam: The Everlasting God

El Roi: The God Who Sees

El Shaddai: God Almighty

Elohim: The Creator

Yahweh: The Self-Existent One

Yahweh-Bore: The LORD Creator

Yahweh-Nissi: The LORD My Banner

Yahweh-Raah: The LORD My Shepherd

Yahweh-Rapha: The LORD That Healeth

Yahweh-Shalom: The LORD Is Peace

Yahweh-Shammah: The LORD Is There

Yahweh-Tsabbaoth: The LORD of Hosts

Yahweh-Tsidkenu: The LORD Our Righteousness

Yahweh-Yireh: The LORD Will Provide

prayer

Everlasting God, thank You for revealing Your character to us through Your names. Thank You for the peace that is ours when we focus on the attributes of who You are. Today, as I live life, let me be sensitive to Your presence and may it impact everything I do. Thank You, Father, for allowing me to know You by name! In Jesus' name, amen.

What Next?

How do each of these names of God affect my life today?

In what areas of my life am I claiming these divine character traits?

Which of these titles for God do I need to depend on most with the challenges I face today?

Day 9

God, Please Do Something!

Rise up, LORD God! Lift up Your hand. Do not forget the afflicted. Why has the wicked person despised God? He says to himself, "You will not demand an account."
—Psalm 10:12-13

When we look around we see a world in chaos:

- 60 million abortions in the United States since the 1973 *Roe v. Wade* Supreme Court decision
- 20–30 million adults and children currently being bought and sold worldwide into commercial sexual servitude, forced labor, and bonded labor
- The legalization of same-sex marriage by the 2015 *Obergefell v. Hodges* Supreme Court decision
- 2 million children exploited every year in the global commercial sex trade

Whether it's the brutal beheading of Christians by ISIS, the abduction of an innocent child, or senseless violence on a helpless neighbor, we are pummeled daily with things that cause righteous anger in our lives. This type of anger is based on our love for God and our neighbor, which is rooted in the great commandment:

He said to him, "Love the Lord your God with all your heart, with all your soul, and with all your mind. This is the greatest and most important command. The second is like it: Love your neighbor as yourself."
—Matthew 22:37-40

Even Jesus became angry about things that contradicted the laws of God (see Mark 3:1–6; 10:13–16; John 2:13–17), but He expects us to handle our anger correctly. That's why the Apostle Paul reminds us in Ephesians 4:26–27 to "Be angry and do not sin. Don't let the sun go down on your anger, and don't give the Devil an opportunity."

Psalm 10 deals with the basic question that comes to mind when we see so much evil in the world: *God, why won't You do something?* The psalmist cries out, "Rise up, Lord God!" He begs the Lord to punish the evildoers. Even in the midst of his anger, however, verse 16 affirms, "The Lord is King forever." This reality allows us to trust that God will bring justice in His time . . . even though we would prefer a shorter timeline.

With so much evil around us, that is a truth we can rely on.

prayer

Jesus, Lover of My Soul, I beg You to bring peace to my heart in the midst of so much evil in the world. Because sin and unrighteousness are all around me, allow me to be angry without sinning, an anger defined by love and not vengeance. Give me a confidence that You will make all things beautiful in Your time (Ecclesiastes 3:11). I ask these things in the powerful name of Jesus. Amen.

What Next?

Compile a list of things that make you angry. Make sure your anger:

- Is an honest reaction against sin as defined by Scripture (Romans 3:23; 1 John 3:4)
- Focuses on evil against God, not on your own rights or preferences
- Is expressed in godly ways and not uncontrolled

Day 10

Fire!

The words of the LORD are pure words, like silver refined in an earthen furnace, purified seven times.

—Psalm 12:6

In all small Mississippi towns, when a siren sang, everyone came outside to look. One Sunday in Wiggins, Mississippi, the siren sang while most of the citizens were in church. The fire chief and many of the volunteer firemen in that small town were members of First Baptist Wiggins, a church I would serve some 20-plus years later, and they left the service to respond to the call. The house that burned belonged to a prominent family in that church, and it burned to the ground. Yet, that family of five faced that adversity through their faith, which was strengthened and refined by that fire.

Sometimes in life, a little fire is a good thing. Fire is used to keep us warm and to toast marshmallows for s'mores. Seriously, who doesn't enjoy sitting beside the fire on a cool fall night with your family and friends? More importantly, fire is used to temper things—to improve them—for better purposes. Things such as taking raw materials and making steel for use in building and highways, heating chemicals to change their properties, and creating new medicines and other materials for the good of mankind. Fire is also used to purify precious metals such as gold and silver. That fire is called the "refiner's fire," and is what the psalmist references in this verse.

God allows us to go through the fire at times. And through those times, He is with us. And though it can be tough, we come out of the situation better for having been in it.

Gerald Crabb wrote these words as the chorus of his anthem "Through the Fire":

𝄋

*Just remember when you're standing in the valley of
decision and the advisory says give in,
Just hold on, our Lord will show up, and He will take
you through the fire again.*

𝄚

God's words are pure—they hold no dross, imperfections, or fallacies.
We can trust them totally.

prayer

Lord, I confess I have struggled with having to go through
the fires of life. I ask forgiveness for that. I thank You for the
pure truth of Your words and the purity of the gift of Your
Son who went through the ultimate fire for my sins. Amen.

What Next?

List times in your life you have been in the fire. What changed in
you when you went through them? Note how God used you before,
during, and after those times.

Record other Scripture passages (there are several in the Book of
Psalms) that talk about the refiner's fire.

$\mathcal{D}ay$ 11

The Biggest Fool of All

The fool says in his heart, "God does not exist." They are
corrupt; they do vile deeds. There is no one who does good.
—Psalm 14:1

I'm perplexed by atheists. The argument that everything came from nothing is utterly illogical, yet those who espouse it try to stake their position on assumed intellectual superiority. A giant "cosmic car crash," known as the "Big Bang," ignites a sprawling universe comprised of more than 2 trillon galaxies. The Milky Way alone is punctuated with more than 1,000,000,000,000, 000,000,000,000 (that's 100 billion) stars. Additionally, a process is ignited that generates human life . . . all from nothing! I don't think so. Psalm 14:1 reminds us that a person who says there is no God is a fool.

I have a friend who is an atheist. Over lunch we've discussed his recently developed views on life and faith. He grew up in our church and has a seminary degree but embraced an atheistic worldview after making some poor decisions and losing his family. I'll give him this: at least he's honest about his unbelief.

Too often Christians say, "We believe," yet live our lives as if there is no God. In effect, we live as functional atheists. Sure, we go to church when it's convenient, read our Bibles and pray when we're in a bind, and take the moral high ground on every social issue imaginable. But we don't really have an intimate relationship with God. We don't share our faith because we're concerned about offending someone. We live our lives just like those who don't believe . . . we just give lip service to God.

Penn Jillette, who is part of the powerhouse magic duo, Penn and Teller, is an atheist who sees the disconnect in what Christians say and the way we live:

I've always said that I don't respect people who don't proselytize. I don't respect that at all. If you believe that there's a heaven and a hell, and people could be going to hell or not getting eternal life, and you think that it's not really worth telling them this because it would make it socially awkward . . . how much do you have to hate somebody to not proselytize? How much do you have to hate somebody to believe everlasting life is possible and not tell them that? I mean, if I believed, beyond the shadow of a doubt, that a truck was coming at you, and you didn't believe that truck was bearing down on you, there is a certain point where I tackle you. And this is more important than that.

Do you really believe what you say you believe? Or is your faith more a badge you wear than a relationship you have? Christian atheists are all around us. They fill our churches, our schools, and our work places. In my case, far too many times I see one staring back at me from my mirror. A Christian living like there is no God? Now that's the biggest fool of all.

prayer

Father, forgive me for claiming to believe in You and yet living like You don't exist. I ask You for a passionate desire to know You more. Allow my life to reflect an intimate, growing relationship with You so that others may see You through me. Amen.

What Next?

Are you a Christian atheist? What message does the way you live your life send to those around you? Do you reflect a passionate belief in God, or are you just going through the motions?

Day 12

How Am I Supposed to Look?

LORD, who can dwell in Your tent? Who can live on Your holy mountain? The one who lives honestly, practices righteousness, and acknowledges the truth in his heart— who does not slander with his tongue, who does not harm his friend or discredit his neighbor, who despises the one rejected by the LORD but honors those who fear the LORD, who keeps his word whatever the cost, who does not lend his money at interest or take a bribe against the innocent—the one who does these things will never be moved.

—Psalm 15:1-5

One of the longest running game shows in American history is *Jeopardy!*, on the air since 1984. Contestants are presented with general knowledge clues in the form of answers and must phrase their responses in the form of questions. You don't succeed at *Jeopardy!* unless you can ask good questions. David understood this dilemma.

Psalm 15 is considered a wisdom psalm. Its offering of words for daily living makes it similar to the books of Proverbs and Ecclesiastes. David begins the psalm by asking the same question in two different ways. "LORD, who can dwell in Your tent?" and "Who can live on Your holy mountain?" He basically is asking, "As worshipper of Yahweh, how am I supposed to look?"

The answer is overwhelming. The true worshipper lives a lifestyle of holiness that is demonstrated in practical terms by honesty and righteousness, having a pure heart, living with integrity, and speaking words that are good and edifying. At its core, a worshipper of Yahweh must take on the attributes of God.

While this sounds impossible, throughout Scripture we see God using imperfect people such as Noah, Abraham, Moses, and Paul. Because of the blood of Jesus, our imperfections and failures can be forgiven, thus allowing us to dwell on the holy mountain of His presence.

prayer

Holy God, I confess the many ways I have failed to live out the things required to dwell in Your presence. Today I ask that You take my heart and purify it, take my tongue and place it under Your control, and fill my mind with thoughts that honor You. Allow my life to be lived in Your presence. In the powerful name of Jesus, amen.

What Next?

Make a list of sins the Holy Spirit has brought to mind as a result of reading Psalm 15, and ask for God's forgiveness.

Identify times throughout your day when you are more susceptible to sin, and set boundaries to protect your heart.

Day 13

An Irresistible Future

LORD, You are my portion and my cup of blessing; You hold my future. The boundary lines have fallen for me in pleasant places; indeed, I have a beautiful inheritance.

—Psalm 16:5-6

On a June night in 1951, a man wearing Victorian era clothing seemed to appear from nowhere in the middle of Times Square in New York City. Startled and confused, the man inadvertently stepped in front of an oncoming taxi and died. The New York City morgue identified the deceased as Rudolph Fentz and found the following items on his person:

- A copper token bearing the name of a local business unknown even to older residents of the area
- A receipt for the care of a horse and the washing of a carriage from a nonexistent livery stable
- About $70 in old paper money
- Business cards with the name Rudolph Fentz and an address on Fifth Avenue
- A letter dated June 1876, 75 years earlier

None of these objects showed signs of aging and provided no help in identifying the man. Fentz was not listed in the address book, his fingerprints were not on record, and he had not been reported missing. Investigators finally located the widow of a Rudolph Fentz Jr., who had died five years before. Mrs. Fentz shared with authorities that her husband's father had disappeared in 1876 at the age of 29, having left the house for an evening walk and never returned.

Whether it's H. G. Wells's *The Time Machine* or the popular 1980s film *Back to the Future*, people are often obsessed with the future. Even this story, although based on a short story by science fiction author Jack Finney, still captures people's attention and frequently shows up as an urban legend on social media. Why? Because the future is uncertain and beyond our control. People are fearful of a moral or economic collapse of our society as well as of terror attacks or a plague that might wipe out civilization. For some this fear is paralyzing. For others, it leaves our spirits in a state of turmoil.

In Psalm 16, the writer is not fearful. In fact, he writes of the future with peace and comfort. He says, "You hold my future. The boundary lines have fallen for me in pleasant places." Jesus also knew our propensity to be anxious about the future.

> *So don't worry, saying, "What will we eat?" or "What will we drink?" or "What will we wear?" For the idolaters eagerly seek all these things, and your heavenly Father knows that you need them. But seek first the kingdom of God and His righteousness, and all these things will be provided for you.*
>
> *—Matthew 6:31-33*

Are you fearful of the future? If so, place it squarely on the shoulders of Jesus. Oswald Chambers wrote, "Let the past sleep, but let it sleep on the bosom of Christ, and go out into the irresistible future with Him." Embrace the irresistible future today!

prayer

Never changing God, I am thankful You are the same yesterday, today, and forever. This promise helps me face the future knowing the God who never changes has my life in His hands. Allow me to embrace this today as I navigate what Your plans are for me. Amen.

What Next?

When you think of the future, what emotions do you experience?

Take a few minutes to read Matthew 6:25-34. What are key lessons in this passage about anxiety?

$\mathcal{D}ay$ 14

Safe and Secure

He makes my feet like the feet of a deer and sets me securely on the heights.

—*Psalm 18:33*

If you've traveled through the national parks of the United States or Canada, you have likely seen many surefooted animals up on the sides of the mountains, grazing along, seemingly oblivious to the world and what is going on around them. There are many of them: elk, moose, goats, bear, antelope, deer. They are beautiful to watch. In Glacier National Park in Montana, as you ride the famous Red Buses up the Going-to-the-Sun Road to Logan Pass, you are glad to leave the driving to the guides and take in the view as the hairpin curves are treacherous! Some of us were fortunate when walking around the visitor center at Logan Pass to see some mountain goats up close and personal. It was amazing—they knew we could not get too close, and if we did, they knew with certainty they were a lot faster than us!

Psalm 18:33 in the King James Version more specifically refers to a hind, or a female deer, most often of the red deer species, who is over three years old. They are *fast*. They are so sure of foot that when running, their back feet hit the same place their front feet had just been. They can easily and quickly reach a higher place on the mountain for food and shelter without concern for another creature catching up with them.

David did a lot of running in his day. He ran after the sheep. He ran away from Saul. He even had to run away from his children at one point. He was often looking for a place to hide. And, though a physically fit young shepherd and warrior, he gave God all the glory for keeping him safe and meeting his needs.

The prophet Habakkuk quotes from this psalm at the end of an elegant discourse with God. He is frustrated with Judah, a nation headed for destruction, but he channels his frustrations into a frank and uplifting conversation with God. Habakkuk 3:19 wraps it up, citing God as the source of his strength and as well as his protector and provider, "Yahweh my Lord is my strength; He makes my feet like those of a deer and enables me to walk on mountain heights!"

prayer

Lord, You are my strength and my salvation. I confess I often do not praise and thank You for daily providing for my needs and securing my safety. Help me to be like David and Habakkuk and give You praise and thanks. Help me stop my complaining. Amen.

What Next?

List in your journal times when you spent your energy and time complaining about your circumstances. Contrast those with times you turned your cares and concerns to the Lord.

Compare Jonah (a complainer) with Habakkuk and David. What do you learn from a look at their attitudes?

Day 15

Loose Lips . . . Unguarded Hearts

May the words of my mouth and the meditation of my heart
be acceptable to You, LORD, my rock and my Redeemer.
—Psalm 19:14

L*oose lips sink ships*, a phrase originating during World War II, reminded Americans to beware of unguarded talk. Too bad Kentucky Congressman Andrew J. May didn't get that memo! After a visit to sites in the Pacific Theater during the summer of 1943, May and other members of the United States House of Representatives returned home to a press conference. May shared a little too much information when he boasted confidence in the safety of American submarines. He explained how the Japanese were setting their depth charges—a type of anti-submarine explosive—to detonate at too shallow depths. This meant the subs could avoid them. The papers reported May's comments, including ones in Hawaii and other Pacific coastal areas. The commander of the US submarine fleet in the Pacific blamed May's indiscretion for the later destruction of ten submarines and the loss of 800 crewmen.

C. S. Lewis called Psalm 19 "the greatest poem in the Psalter and one of the greatest lyrics in the world." The opening verse extols God's glory as revealed in creation: "The heavens declare the glory of God, and the sky proclaims the work of His hands." The psalm ends with verse 14, one of the most quoted Scripture passages. As a worshipper, David understood the importance of guarding our mouths and hearts. Not only do our words and our innermost thoughts reflect our walk with the Lord, they also determine our ability to connect with God in worship.

The words we use matter to God. Do you use your words to encourage? Or are your words saturated with negativity and anger? With our words, we can bless or curse . . . exalt or destroy. Several years ago, someone gave me three questions to use as a filter for my words. When potential comments are passed through this filter, I've found there's often no need for me to speak:

Does it need to be said?

Does it need to be said now?

Does it need to be said by me?

On what type of things do you focus your mind? What are your thought patterns throughout the day? What are you allowing into your mind? The things on which we meditate and focus will determine our spiritual condition. Toxicity generates sickness.

prayer

Oh Lord, my Rock and my Redeemer, may my words today be pleasing in Your sight. Protect my heart by allowing me to focus on things that draw me closer to You. To You be all the glory. Amen.

What Next?

How would you describe the true state of your heart? What does it look like to guard your heart?

Do you use your words to lift up or tear down? Do others interpret your speech as a weapon or a balm?

Day 16

Are You Anointed?

Now I know that the LORD gives victory to His anointed;
He will answer him from His holy heaven with mighty
victories from His right hand. Some take pride in chari-
ots, and others in horses, but we take pride in the name of
Yahweh our God.

—*Psalm 20:6-7*

Psalms 20 and 21 are often combined into what we know as Warfare Psalms. Psalm 20 was written as a prayer for the king of Israel before he went into battle. Psalm 21 was sung in celebration after the battle ended. Throughout history, music played a central role in warfare. One of the earliest examples of this is found in Joshua 6 when trumpets (ram horns) were used against the city of Jericho:

Early on the seventh day, they started at dawn and
marched around the city seven times in the same way.
That was the only day they marched around the city seven
times. After the seventh time, the priests blew the trumpets,
and Joshua said to the people, "Shout! For the LORD has
given you the city. . . . So the people shouted, and the trum-
pets sounded. When they heard the blast of the trumpet,
the people gave a great shout, and the wall collapsed. The
people advanced into the city, each man straight ahead,
and they captured the city.

—*Joshua 6:15-16, 20*

It wasn't music, or even shouting, that brought down Jericho's four-story walls. Instead, it was God working through his anointed servant Joshua (Numbers 27:18-22). The victory was won not because of methodologies but through obedience, faithfulness, and God's gracious blessing. Psalm 20:6 reminds us the Lord "gives victory to His anointed." What does that mean? It means through the grace and mercy of God we have been enabled and empowered to do God's will. As believers we are a royal priesthood called to praise God and share His love with a lost world:

> *But you are a chosen race, a royal priesthood, a holy nation, a people for His possession, so that you may proclaim the praises of the One who called you out of darkness into His marvelous light.*
>
> *—1 Peter 2:9*

As worshippers, far too often we rely on our own strength to take us into the spiritual battles of life. At the end of the day it will not be chariots and horses that prevail but rather the contrite heart that has been anointed for victory by God Himself.

prayer

King of the universe, thank You for anointing me through the Holy Spirit to carry out Your will. I ask that You allow Your presence to fill me today so I may worship You in truth and spirit and reflect Your presence to everyone I encounter. Remove any thought from my mind that impairs me from becoming more like You. Thank You for Your Son Jesus, in whose name I pray. Amen.

What Next?

In your own words, write what it means in your life to be anointed by God.

Identify three specific areas in your life in which you are fighting spiritual or physical battles.

List ways you can rely on God's strength to fight those battles.

Day 17

We Will Praise You

Be exalted, Lord, in Your strength; we will sing and praise Your might.

—Psalm 21:13

I grew up a fan of professional wrestling. Now I'm not talking about the collegiate or Olympic-type competition. I like the fake, entertainment-driven genre, featuring names such as Andre the Giant, Cowboy Bill Watts, The Spoiler, and my personal favorite, the Junkyard Dog. Many memorable times were spent with my grandfather watching these bouts play out on Saturday afternoon TV.

In the mid1980s, we decided to attend a night of "wrastlin'" at the state fair. All of our favorites were headlining the card that evening, so we arrived early to take in the full experience. About halfway through the night, my little brother, Duran, slipped down to taunt some of the bad guys as they entered the arena . . . and that's where the fun started.

As the spotlights hit that part of the building, none other than the *The Great Kabuki*, archnemesis of Dusty Rhodes, made his appearance. Kabuki was a sight to behold. With long, unruly hair and a ghastly painted face, Kabuki looked like he had stepped out of a classic horror movie. As Kabuki made his entrance, Duran yelled and jeered as Kabuki made his way down the rope line. At that moment, Kabuki jumped across the rope line, grabbed at Duran, and spit his famous green "Asian mist" into the air. Duran, somewhat large for a kid his age, ran up the steps of the Mississippi Coliseum and exited the building, setting multiple new state track records in the process!

The strength of Kabuki was fake—all theatrics designed to entertain. Not so when it comes to God. Psalm 21, the second of the Warfare Psalms, is a celebratory song of praise after the king returned victorious from battle. This is not fake strength. Though more battles will come, they exuberantly praise God for what He has done in the past, is doing in the present, and will do in the future.

In life, praise doesn't always come easily. It's in those times I'm reminded that God's strength and might never changes. Our worship of God is not dependent on circumstances or events. It is a choice we make to focus on the immutable and eternal character of the King of Glory. In Acts 16, Paul and Silas are thrown into prison after casting a demon from a slave girl. In less than ideal circumstances, they chose to worship:

> *About midnight Paul and Silas were praying and singing hymns to God, and the prisoners were listening to them. Suddenly there was such a violent earthquake that the foundations of the jail were shaken, and immediately all the doors were opened, and everyone's chains came loose.*
> —*Acts 16:25–26*

May our worship reflect the *real* strength of the God we serve . . . not something fake and contrived.

prayer

Unchangeable God, I praise You today regardless of the circumstances through which I'm walking. Help me connect with Your heart. Protect me from the lies of the enemy, and demonstrate Your strength in all aspects of my life. In Jesus' name. Amen.

What Next?

Are there areas in your life where you use fake strength to address the challenges and circumstances life presents you? List them.

Read Psalm 21 in its entirety. Like the Psalmist, what are specific ways God has blessed you?

Day 18

The Crucifixion Psalm

*My God, my God, why have You forsaken me? Why are
You so far from my deliverance and from my words of
groaning? . . . Everyone who sees me mocks me; they sneer
and shake their heads: "He relies on the LORD; let Him
rescue him; let the LORD deliver him, since He takes pleasure in him." . . . They divided my garments among themselves, and they cast lots for my clothing. . . . They will
come and tell a people yet to be born about His righteousness—what He has done.*

— Psalm 22:1–31

As a child, I loved watching the network television presentation of George Stevens's epic film, *The Greatest Story
Ever Told*, with my family. Back in the day, before DVDs,
Netflix, and DVR, my family gathered around televisions every
Easter to watch the life of Christ play out in full color, complete with
wise men, the Crucifixion . . . and even John Wayne as the centurion
soldier. Eventually other films were produced with titles such as
*Jesus of Nazareth, The Gospel According to Matthew, The Passion
of the Christ*, and *Son of God*. Each, in its own way, provides viewers
with a connection to the story of Jesus Christ. But for Jesus, His life
is not *merely* a story.

Too often, we view Jesus as a superhero character, more akin to
Batman or the Man of Steel, than to the reality of who He is: the
Lamb of God. His virgin birth is viewed as hyperbole, His miracles
as fairy tales, and His death as a tragic ending found only in the
latest Hollywood blockbuster. Our view of His story is evident in our
approach to worship each week. Unprepared and if convenient, we
show up at church and go through the motions singing songs, reading Scripture, and reciting prayers, but we remain the same. Our
lives are not changed. Our problem is we *know* the story—maybe too
well—but have failed to experience the *reality* of who Jesus is.

Many biblical scholars agree that on Friday, April 3, AD 33, Jesus of Nazareth was crucified on a hill outside of Jerusalem. While the date may be open to discussion, what happened three days later is not. On that first Easter morning, Jesus Christ came forth from the tomb victorious over sin, death, and the grave and, with that victory, offering salvation to all who will accept Him as Lord and Savior.

In the midst of your hectic schedule, don't miss the significance of what happened in Jerusalem more than 2,000 years ago. While children's stories often begin with the words, "Once upon a time," the events of the first Easter took place in "the fulness of the time" (Galatians 4:4 KJV). One phrase sets up fairy tales; the other introduces the "Lamb of God who takes away the sin of the world!" (John 1:29). There is a huge difference! May His death and Resurrection be real to us.

prayer

King of glory, forgive me for the superficial way I've approached the reality of Your death. Allow Your suffering and pain to become real in my life. Amen.

What Next?

Read Psalm 22 and the Apostle John's account of the Crucifixion (John 19). Intentionally visualize the reality Jesus experienced and focus on the reality of His suffering. Allow yourself to experience the pain and emotion of the price paid for us at Calvary. Remember, it is more than a story!

Day 19

Herding Cats

The LORD is my shepherd; there is nothing I lack.
—Psalm 23:1

T hough we most often associate Psalm 23 with consolation during times of turmoil and grief, let's look at it from the point of view of God's provision regardless of circumstance.

As you might imagine, there are many stories from the nearly 50 years of Carols by Candlelight, the annual sharing of the gospel through music, drama, and other art forms each Christmas at my church, First Jackson in Jackson, Mississippi. And, you don't put 400-plus singers, instrumentalists, kids, stage crew, and audiovisual folks in a room for nine out of ten consecutive days without some form of mental or physical breakdown from time to time. One traditional element of Carols is the candlelight processional. Our production team logistics leader refers to it as "herding cats," an idiom famously utilized in the award-winning commercial for technology services company Electronic Data Systems (EDS) for Super Bowl XXXIV. The premise is how to control the uncontrollable. If you need a laugh, this commercial is still available on YouTube.

Herding cats is not much different from herding sheep—it's never simple or easy! But unlike cats, sheep *need* someone to herd them (just as choir members do for Carols!), to provide for them, to comfort them, to be present for them, to meet their every need. The shepherd fills that role. David knew about sheep and the role of the shepherd from personal experience, and, from the depth of that experience, he penned this psalm. Some think David may have written Psalm 23 during his shepherding days, but it was more likely penned retrospectively during the time of war caused by the rebellion of his son Absalom (2 Samuel 15–18). David left Jerusalem to spare the city and her people during this time and did some wilderness wandering. Unfortunately, it came down to a fight between Absalom and his followers and David and his. And despite everything, when Absalom died, David grieved the loss of his son.

In Psalm 23:2–3, we sense the calm the Shepherd brought to the chaos surrounding David: "He lets me lie down in green pastures; He leads me beside quiet waters. He renews my life; He leads me along the right paths for His name's sake."

Did you catch that last line? *He leads me along the right paths for His name's sake.* He is herding us where He wants us to go—where we are protected, our needs met, where our will is aligned with His for us. We must choose to follow, and when we do, His provision will sustain us. And when we think it cannot get any better, we hear verse 6 as the Shepherd commits to provide for all our days. I see this promise as one for me in my earthly life and for eternity in my choice to follow the Shepherd: "Only goodness and faithful love will pursue me all the days of my life, and I will dwell in the house of the LORD as long as I live."

prayer

Lord, forgive me for trying to lead myself. Today, I give myself to You fully. Amen.

What Next?

Read 2 Samuel 15–18 and record the decisions David made during the chaos (cats running wild!) around him. Note whose well-being was first and foremost in his mind.

Explore Psalm 23 verse by verse, recording how God met your needs during your life's journey as He similarly met David's.

Day 20

Mine!

The earth and everything in it, the world and its inhabitants, belong to the LORD; for He laid its foundation on the seas and established it on the rivers.

—Psalm 24:1-2

I am a Disney fanatic. If something is Disney branded, most likely I have seen it or been to it. There is a lot of human nature embedded in Disney productions, especially in the movies. One of my favorites is *Finding Nemo*, which chronicles the misadventures of a clown fish, Marlin, as he tries to find his son Nemo. At one point, Marlin encounters a group of seagulls. When the seagulls see Marlin, they see food, and they go into a frenzy shouting, "Mine!" "Mine!" "Mine!" Those cries of possession (for something that they wanted but did nothing to acquire or create) follow you long after the movie is over.

Trying to possess something we have no right to is human nature. When we see something powerful or beneficial—or maybe just shiny and attractive—we desire to touch it, claim it. In Scripture, the Ark of the Covenant was just such an item, drawing people to it, despite warnings from God.

Many believe David wrote Psalm 24 to celebrate the return of the Ark of the Covenant to the Tabernacle, its holy place, during his reign. The Ark represented to the Jewish people the presence of God, thus where the Ark traveled, worship occurred as the people celebrated God. From the beginning, God gave many instructions for the handling of the Ark—it was not to be taken lightly by the Jews, and when it was, such as when the Philistines returned it to the Jews (1 Samuel 4), disaster occurred. The Philistines did not know how the Ark was to be handled and suffered because of it. The Jews did know what to do, but due to carelessness or obstinacy ("God, we have a better idea on how to move this thing."), they too suffered before David finally got the move under control and headed back up

Mount Zion to the Tabernacle. To disobey God's instructions was representative of violating God Himself.

In setting up this psalm, David made sure the people acknowledged that everything belongs to God. Not just heavenly things—everything. Holding on to things was not God honoring. God's ownership was not limited to the world itself—crops and animals and material things. His ownership of the world and everything in it included His people—all the people. There was no place for "Mine!" "Mine!" "Mine!" as they prepared for worship. The psalm goes on to specify the qualifications of those who could ascend the hill and approach the holiest of places. You had to be clean—pure of heart, honest, and obedient. If you were, you could go, and God would bless you.

Are you singing the song of "Mine!" "Mine!" "Mine!" with the seagulls or have you released to God all that is His? Is your heart pure so you can approach Him? Think about it.

prayer

Lord, I confess I hold on to possessions and even people as stuff that I control and own. Forgive me for this, and show me how to release these to You so that I can approach You and worship. Amen.

What Next?

Make a list of the things you cling to as yours and yours alone ("Mine!").

Journal your prayers of confession to release each one to Him.

Day 21

Who Are Your Heroes?

The LORD is good and upright; therefore He shows sinners the way. He leads the humble in what is right and teaches them His way.

—Psalm 25:8-9

Everyone loves heroes! We tend to put people on pedestals and exalt them. Truthfully, our heroes are ordinary people who excelled at something . . . they're really no different from us. Those who impacted my life the most were humble, everyday people. None would consider themselves "great," but through their commitment to serving our Lord they embodied greatness. Let me share a few of my heroes . . .

Travis Drury was a member of West Union Baptist Church, the first church where I filled a full-time position. Travis became a Christian in his late 50s. He had little education and had worked and lived hard his entire life. After meeting Jesus, however, his priorities took an immediate shift. Travis met with me to explain he couldn't read but was enrolled in a reading class so he could study his Bible. He also loved music and wanted to sing in the choir. Each week I gave Travis his music to take to his reading class, and each week he showed up in choir . . . and sang every word with a big smile! Though uneducated, Travis was wise enough to understand the importance of worship. Travis Drury is one of my heroes.

Many of us take things for granted. Not so with Bob Sigrest. Bob was a deacon at First Jackson and a faithful member of our choir for many years. Over time, macular degeneration robbed Bob of his sight. Honestly, at first I didn't realize this because Bob was always (Wednesdays, Sundays, and every special program) in choir. In 2005, in the aftermath of Hurricane Katrina, our worship ministry traveled to New Orleans to present a concert. I sat near Bob on the bus and noticed he was holding a piece of paper within three inches of his face. Bob had typed the lyrics to each song, enlarged them to at least a 35-point font, and was memorizing his music. Although legally blind, Bob found a way to worship. Bob Sigrest is one of my heroes.

When I met James Foster, he was in his early 90s, and the years had taken their toll. In fact, Mr. Foster could barely get around. He shuffled with the aid of a walker and could hardly make eye contact because of the curvature of his spine caused by arthritis. Getting anywhere was a challenge . . . but Mr. Foster *never* missed choir. Most nights I passed Mr. Foster being assisted into a car long after everyone else was gone. While others complained about standing too long or missed choir for a variety of reasons, Mr. Foster was always there. A career missionary for more than 30 years, Mr. Foster understood the importance of worship in his life. James Foster is one of my heroes.

There are unsung heroes all around us! Each week they sacrificially give their time and fill their places, not because it's easy but because God has called them to do so. Who's your hero?

prayer

Gracious God, teach me to walk with a humble spirit. Show me the things You would have me do, speak through me the words You would have me say, and fill my mind with the thoughts You would have me think. Be glorified in my life today. Amen.

What's Next?

What has God called you to do? Are you faithful to that calling? Make a list of the heroes around you who are consistent in their Christian walk in spite of difficulties. Take it from a guy who has seen some real heroes: our best, what God deserves, is not always easy.

Day 22

Look in My Eyes

My heart says this about You, "You are to seek My face."
LORD, I will seek Your face.

—Psalm 27:8

After nearly 30 years of marriage, my wife Wendy doesn't need to say anything to communicate to me exactly what's she's thinking. Her eyes convey the message clearly. Simply by catching her glance, I can tell if she's annoyed, content, angry, or happy. With just a slight shift of her eyebrow, she lets me know if something I said was well received or went too far. She speaks to me without saying a word.

While phones, texting, and video calls are great when I'm away from home, nothing—and I mean nothing—replaces seeing her face in person. Several years ago, I was on a missions trip in the Ukraine with no way to communicate back home. At night, I would close my eyes and remember every trait of her appearance—her smile, the contour of her chin, the shape of her eyes. I know those attributes because I know her intimately. After all, she's the love of my life. Even when isolated from her actual presence, I can recall every aspect of her countenance in detail.

In Psalm 27 we find David running from Saul. His life is in danger, and his enemies are closing in. David was in need of an intimate encounter with God. In desperation he cries out, "LORD, I will seek Your face." Like David, eventually each of us will find ourselves in a place that causes us to embrace God in total abandon. It's in those "God, please show me your presence" moments that we learn to seek His face . . . every contour . . . every detail. So, what does it take to encounter the presence of the Holy God?

> **Passion**—We need a relentless desire to know God in the fullness of who He is. "How lovely is Your dwelling place, LORD of Hosts. I long and yearn for the courts of the LORD; my heart and flesh cry out for the living God" (Psalm 84:1-2).

Prayer—Our passion for God drives us to desire continual conversations with Him. "But when you pray, go into your private room, shut your door, and pray to your Father who is in secret. And your Father who sees in secret will reward you" (Matthew 6:6).

Bible Study—Our knowledge of God is directly connected to our study of His Word. "Now if I have indeed found favor in Your sight, please teach me Your ways, and I will know You and find favor in Your sight" (Exodus 33:13).

Meditation—We must exclusively focus on God. "May the words of my mouth and the meditation of my heart be acceptable to You, LORD, my rock and my Redeemer" (Psalm 19:14).

Unlike Moses, whose ability to view the presence of God was limited to the Law, we have unrestricted access to His face under the blood of Jesus: "We all, with unveiled faces, are looking as in a mirror at the glory of the Lord and are being transformed into the same image from glory to glory; this is from the Lord who is the Spirit" (2 Corinthians 3:18). Seek His face, memorize every detail, and take on the attributes of the King of glory!

prayer

Lord, thank You for Your presence in my life. Allow me to experience the contours of Your presence and for Your attributes to be reflected in me. Thank You for Jesus, who gives me access to You today. Amen.

What Next?

Review the four keys for seeking God's face. Commit today to implement them in your life.

Day 23
It's All Around Us

Ascribe to Yahweh, you heavenly beings, ascribe to the
LORD glory and strength. Ascribe to Yahweh the glory
due His name; worship Yahweh in the splendor of His
holiness. . . . In His temple all cry, "Glory!"

—Psalm 29:1-2; 9

David was no stranger to nature. As a young shepherd boy he spent many nights on the hillsides of Bethlehem guarding his father's sheep. As a hunter he killed both lions and bears. As king he no doubt lavished in the natural beauty of his kingdom. In fact, David's love for creation is evident throughout the psalms. With poetic beauty, he describes the majesty of God in all the earth, a God who set His glory among the heavens and stars. What was David's response to the God of creation? Worship.

This is evident in Psalm 29 as he reflects on the majesty, wonder, and power of God in nature. Caught in a major thunderstorm, David hears God's mighty voice in the rumble of thunder. While the storm rages, the winds release their mighty strength as lightning flashes around him. David is overcome with the power of God in nature. Power. Splendor. Strength.

On a summer day in the mid1880s, Carl Boberg, a young Swedish preacher and journalist, was caught in a thunderstorm. Taking shelter, he watched in awe at the power of the storm. Lightning flashed, filling the darkened, afternoon sky. Suddenly, it was over. As quickly as the storm appeared, it dissipated.

Later, as Boberg continued to reflect on the majesty, awe, and glory of God in that storm, he penned these words:

O Lord my God! When I in awesome wonder,
Consider all the works thy hand hath made.
I see the stars, I hear the rolling thunder,

Thy power throughout the universe displayed.
Then sings my soul, my Savior God, to thee;
How great thou art, how great thou art!

God clearly and indisputably reveals His presence through creation . . . and our response to that revelation must be worship. The Apostle Paul understood this, saying in Romans 1:20, "For His invisible attributes, that is, His eternal power and divine nature, have been clearly seen since the creation of the world, being understood through what He has made. As a result, people are without excuse."

His glory is all around us. Let's worship!

prayer

All powerful King of creation, I am overwhelmed by Your majesty and grandeur. Allow me to hear Your voice in the midst of the storm. Today, as I live my life, allow Your presence to define my character. Make Your presence real to me today. Amen.

What Next?

Set aside 15 minutes today to take a walk. Look for ways God is displaying His power and majesty to you through His creation.

Day 24

From Lament to Gladness

You turned my lament into dancing; You removed my sackcloth and clothed me with gladness, so that I can sing to You and not be silent. LORD my God, I will praise You forever.

—Psalm 30:11–12

A devout Christian, Horatio Spafford lost everything in the great Chicago Fire of 1871, an event that had been preceded a year earlier by the death of his son. Unfortunately, things would still get worse.

Spafford and his family planned a European trip in 1873. In November of that year, due to unexpected last-minute business developments, Spafford was detained from setting sail with his family but sent his wife and four daughters on ahead as scheduled on the steamer *Ville du Havre*. On November 21 the *Ville du Havre* was struck by the English vessel *Lochearn* and sank in 12 minutes. Of the five members of his family, only Spafford's wife was among the survivors.

Spafford immediately left Chicago to join his grieving wife. As his ship approached the area of the ocean where the ship carrying his daughters had sunk, Spafford's grief-filled prayers gave way to a sense of peace and understanding. He then penned these words:

When peace, like a river, attendeth my way,
When sorrows like sea billows roll;
Whatever my lot, thou hast taught me to say,
It is well, it is well with my soul.

Let's face it. Eventually we all travel through a valley's darkness—the death of a loved one, an unexpected diagnosis, a wayward child, a failed dream. The reasons are countless, but make no mistake. You are in mourning. You wear sackcloth and ashes. Worship seems a distant memory. You have no desire to dance . . . maybe never again.

Jairus understood your despair. He was a leader of the synagogue, yet his 12-year-old daughter was at death's door. As he pled for Jesus to come and heal her, he was informed she had died. But Jesus came anyway: "Then He took the child by the hand and said to her, *'Talitha koum!'* (which is translated, 'Little girl, I say to you, get up!'). Immediately the girl got up and began to walk. (She was 12 years old.) At this they were utterly astounded" (Mark 5:41–42). Cue the music . . . it's time to dance! If you're mourning today, it's all right to grieve for a season—in fact, it's necessary. God graciously gives us time to mourn loss and navigate sorrow. Remember, however, in Jesus, sorrow is temporary. Joy comes in the morning! A glad reunion day is coming when every tear will be wiped away.

prayer

Dear Lord, help me to dance, and help me to encourage others to dance so we may sing Your praises and give thanks to You forever! Amen.

What Next?

Have you experienced an event in your life that stole your joy? Describe the emotions experienced when your lament was turned to dancing.

Day 25

A Manger in the Shadow of the Cross

Into Your hand I entrust my spirit; You redeem me, LORD, God of truth.

—Psalm 31:5

The story of Jesus' birth is amazing. As a young child, I learned about it in Sunday School and heard it told each year in our home. As a minister of music for more than 30 years, I've helped tell this story every Christmas. In fact, because I've attended so many Christmas musicals, cantatas, and children's pageants, I feel I know the shepherds on a first name basis. Unfortunately, unless we are careful, we can get so familiar with the events surrounding Christmas that we miss the purpose of Christmas.

God created us to have a relationship with Him, one in which we trust Him entirely with our spirit and our lives. But sin creates a barrier to that relationship, resulting in an empty place in our hearts. Looking around, you will see people trying to fill this empty place with different things. It might be money, fame, or relationships . . . but nothing works. At the end of the day that empty place remains.

But God had a plan. Scripture tells us in the fullness of time, or when the time was just right, God sent His Son to this earth to be born in a manger. This is the part of the story we know so well, but the story doesn't end there. For the next 33 years, Jesus walked this earth, ministering to those around Him, healing the lame, giving sight to the blind, raising the dead. Then, in the greatest display of love in the history of the universe, this Babe of Bethlehem died on the Cross of Calvary so our sins could be forgiven. Because of His death, the sin barrier was destroyed and the empty place in our lives can be filled. This is the purpose of Christmas. Without His death, burial, and Resurrection, the Babe in the manger is just another story.

The lyrics of the English carol, "What Child Is This?" beautifully juxtapose the Cross with the manger, highlighting the truth the Christ Child was born to die:

Nails, spear shall pierce Him through,
The cross be borne for me, for you.
Hail, hail the Word made flesh,
The Babe, the Son of Mary.

prayer

Christ of Bethlehem, today I celebrate the hope-filled life I live because of You. I offer my worship to You because You are my blessed Savior, my crucified Lord, and my risen King! I confess that at times the reality of Your sacrifice is overshadowed by my self-centeredness. Forgive me and allow me to experience the glory of who You are. In Jesus' name. Amen.

What Next?

The reality that Bethlehem pointed directly to Calvary is difficult to process. Take time to read and reflect on Luke 2 and John 19. Make a list of emotions Mary might have experienced knowing she was giving birth to the Messiah. Remember, without the Cross, Christmas is just another birthday.

Day 26

Wasting Away

When I kept silent, my bones became brittle from my groaning all day long. For day and night Your hand was heavy on me; my strength was drained as in the summer's heat. Then I acknowledged my sin to You and did not conceal my iniquity. I said, "I will confess my transgressions to the LORD," and You took away the guilt of my sin.

—Psalm 32:3–5

There is a tale of the eighteenth century King of Prussia Frederick the Great visiting a Berlin prison. On his arrival, all the prisoners fell to their knees proclaiming their innocence. Only one man remained standing. Upon being questioned by the king, the prisoner admitted to his guilt and said he deserved his punishment. The story goes that Frederick immediately ordered the jailer, "Release this guilty wretch at once. I will not have him kept in this prison where he will corrupt all the fine innocent people who occupy it."

Human nature causes us to use every device, including denial, avoidance, and transference, at our disposal to delay the inevitable consequences of our sin. Doing so, however, comes at a high price. In Psalm 32, David describes the effects of God's hand of conviction on his life, as well as the physical consequences of attempting to conceal his sin. As worshippers, unconfessed sin blocks access to God, shutting down our ability to commune with Him. But then comes the joy of forgiveness . . .

How joyful is the one whose transgression is forgiven, whose sin is covered! How joyful is the man the LORD does not charge with sin and in whose spirit is no deceit!

—Psalm 32:1–2

Tradition states that the early Christian theologian Augustine loved Psalm 32 so much he had it inscribed on the walls of his room so that every time he got out of bed he would be reminded of its truth. For believers the greatest joy comes from knowing that we stand before the King of heaven forgiven and without condemnation.

prayer

Oh Holy One, I beg today that You will give me the courage to honestly confess my sins and turn from my evil way. I pray that You will restore the joy of my salvation through Your forgiveness and that You will renew my spirit with joy and peace. Thank You for Your promise to blot out my transgressions through the blood of Jesus, in whose name I pray. Amen.

What Next?

Reflect on these Scripture passages, and paraphrase them in your own words:

> *Therefore repent and turn back, so that your sins may be wiped out, that seasons of refreshing may come from the presence of the Lord.*
> —*Acts 3:19*

> *"Come, let us discuss this," says the LORD. "Though your sins are like scarlet, they will be as white as snow; though they are as red as crimson, they will be like wool."*
> —*Isaiah 1:18*

> *As far as the east is from the west, so far has He removed our transgressions from us.*
> —*Psalm 103:12*

Day 27

Skillful Worship

Sing a new song to Him; play skillfully on the strings, with a joyful shout.

—Psalm 33:3

Scripture instructs us to sing skillfully. Unfortunately, too many times we as worshippers are guilty of standing before our congregations grossly unprepared for the task to which we've been assigned. Sometimes it's because of a lack of training . . . other times it's simply an unwillingness to pay the price required by adequate training and rehearsal. In either case, the results are usually less than desirable.

I've often said that as a worship pastor, there aren't many things worse than dealing with a musician who doesn't understand his or her own limitations. For example, during the early years of my ministry, every Christian soprano in America bought the books and launched their best Sandi Patti impersonation in their churches. While many of these folks loved Sandi, they had failed to acquire the skills needed to effectively sing her music. The results were often memorable but for all the wrong reasons. It shouldn't be this way!

My own life is no exception. Although I had a clear call from God to be a worship pastor, when I arrived at New Orleans Seminary I did so with limited skills. In fact, limited is a pretty gross overstatement. Although I had taken two years of piano as a young boy, my keyboard skills were marginal at best. I had no background in music theory and had only been part of a choir for a few years in high school and college. Truth is, I could barely read music. This resulted in me being advised on two different occasions while in seminary to change my degree program to an area other than music. But I didn't. The call on my life to be a minister of music outweighed other people's opinions, but I knew to be successful I'd have to improve my musical skills.

As a result, I spent the next years studying voice, piano, and conducting . . . and I improved! Now don't get me wrong, I'm still not the greatest musician out there but the Lord has blessed my efforts to improve. More importantly, in His sovereignty He allows me to use those skills to lead people to His throne each week. That simple fact brings me to my knees every single day.

The truth is, we serve an excellent God, and we should do so in an excellent manner. That doesn't mean perfection, but it does mean sharpening our skills and abilities to the highest level possible. It means giving Him our best. When that happens, we can stand before our congregations and play or sing knowing we are offering an act of worship worthy of a God who gave us His only Son. This in itself compels me to offer the best I have. After all . . . He deserves it!

prayer

Dear Lord, thank You for the gift of music in my life and for those who have worked hard to play and sing skillfully for You. Allow me to pursue excellence with the gifts You've given me. Forgive me for the times I've presented an offering of praise that cost me nothing. Allow me to give You my best. Amen.

What's Next?

In what areas of your life has the Lord called you to "play skillfully"? Have you given your best to perfect the gifts He's given you? How can you improve your sacrifice of praise?

Day 28

Random Access

I sought the LORD, and He answered me and delivered me
from all my fears.

—Psalm 34:4

One of my friends is very intentional in her approach to work, life, friends, family—well, to anything. Thirteen years ago, on a warm night in May, she received news that, over time, caused her to be less methodical in her approach to life—that "C" word—cancer. That night, however, she randomly opened her Bible seeking comfort and immediate peace for the situation she found herself in. Her Bible fell open to Psalm 34:4.

Psalm 34 is one of nine Alphabetical Psalms written as an acrostic of the Hebrew alphabet. David, though the anointed King of Israel (1 Samuel 16:13) for some time, was on the run. And while running, he did some pretty stupid things at times. One of those is found in 1 Samuel 21 when David flees Saul, fearing for his life, and runs to the mortal enemy of Israel, the Philistines. His encounter was with Achish, also referenced as Abimelech, the King of Gath, whose soldiers correctly identified David, the Warrior King.

David, in his fear, reacted impulsively and certainly out of character. Instead of seeking God, he took on the persona of a mentally ill man. And Achish fell for it. Achish chased him off, saying, in verse 15: "Do I have such a shortage of crazy people that you brought this one to act crazy around me? Is this one going to come into my house?"

David later penned Psalm 34, realizing God's hand in his rescue. My friend, in her battle with cancer, realized this verse pointed to a required reliance on the Lord in all things, cancer related or not, life-altering or not.

Psalm 34 is filled with how God saves His people who seek Him. Nowhere, however, does it say His people are exempt from suffering and challenges. That list of nonexempt folks included His own Son Jesus. Psalm 34:19–20 prophesies what is in store for Him (fulfilled in John 19:33): "Many adversities come to the one who is righteous, but the LORD delivers him from them all. He protects all his bones; not one of them is broken."

When you react to a circumstance of life, do you thank God for walking you through the journey, whether that journey is one of your choosing or not? Neither my friend nor David chose the journeys though they did choose their responses to what happened. In our most random of moments, God always has a lifeline extended. It is up to us to grab it.

prayer

Lord, in my random moments when I thrash around for an immediate solution, remind me with clarity to look at You. Forgive me when I am slow or even sometimes completely fail to do that. Amen.

What Next?

Read Psalm 34. List the points in the Psalm that can serve as encouragement to you and to others.

Read John 19. Identify how Jesus reacted to the stressful situation of His life.

$\mathcal{D}ay$ 29

Let the People Sing

*I will praise You in the great congregation; I will exalt
You among many people.*

—Psalm 35:18

In 1989 my wife Wendy and I attended our first Church Music
Week at Ridgecrest Conference Center outside Asheville, North
Carolina. It was a life-changing experience. Each day more than
2,000 church musicians filled Spilman Auditorium for incredible
times of worship. There was a huge choir, orchestra, and amazing soloists, but the defining characteristic was the congregational singing.

In this same location in the 1940s, legendary Southern Baptist
music leader B. B. McKinney launched training programs to equip
church musicians to lead their churches in worship. Now, half a
century later, that legacy continued. For a full week, service after
service, a virtual who's who of church music leaders led the people
in worship. Wesley Forbis, William J. Reynolds, James Woodward
. . . these men were not solo artists. In fact, I never heard them sing
a note. The impact they had on my life, however, was immeasurable.
During that week, they modeled the role of the congregation as
the choir, demonstrating how to utilize dynamic contrasts, instru-
mental variety, and tempo changes with hymns to enhance their
effectiveness. I learned that week the people were supposed to be
participants, not mere spectators.

In later years, others invested in my life underscoring the central
role of the congregation—folks like Graham Smith, who modeled
how to lead with passion, energy, and excitement, and Benjamin
Harlan, who introduced me to the concept of reframing an old
hymn to make it fresh and relevant. Many others reinforced the
truth found in Psalm 35:18: there's something special about lifting
up praise to God in the midst of a great congregation.

For the nearly 1,000 years leading up to Martin Luther's 95
Theses, the church prohibited congregational singing. Leaders such

as Martin Luther and John Calvin restored congregational song to the people, a major component of the Reformation that swept across Europe in the sixteenth century. Unfortunately, far too many churches have digressed to a quasi-pre-Reformation era approach to worship. We have reassigned the congregation as passive observers, with songs being too high to sing or rhythmically unattainable. The musicians on the platform have taken the role of professional worshippers, often forcing a performance-driven model at the exclusion of the people in the congregation. As a result, the people sit, watch, and go home robbed of the opportunity to lift their voices in corporate worship. No wonder people complain about the music. The hard reality is people don't hate worship—they just hate the way we do it! We've taken away their voice and somehow expect them to be happy about it. Shame on us.

In Colossians 3:16, the Apostle Paul gave specific instructions on the role of music in the life of the Christian: "Let the message about the Messiah dwell richly among you, teaching and admonishing one another in all wisdom, and singing psalms, hymns, and spiritual songs, with gratitude in your hearts to God." Today, why don't you take this literally? Lift up your voice and sing the riches of His love!

prayer

Father, thank You for placing a song in my heart and allowing me to use it as vehicle to carry my praise to Your ears. Forgive me for the times I've sat in silence instead of voicing my praise in the midst of a great congregation. Amen.

What Next?

Take a few minutes to list the five songs that have taught you about God and His character.

Commit to sing with enthusiasm this week in corporate worship.

Day 30

Worrywarts

Trust in the LORD and do what is good; dwell in the land and live securely. Take delight in the LORD, and He will give you your heart's desires.

—Psalm 37:3-4

We all know at least one worrywart. Very likely there is at least one in your immediate family. It is possible you are that person! From my family experience, the prime worrywart is the one least likely to want to wait on anything.

The Bible has a lot to say about worry. The best passage may be Luke 12:22–26. Jesus is talking to His disciples about worry, telling them even the needs of the birds and flowers are cared for in detail by the Father. He is emphasizing that needs are handled by faith. (Note: I said *needs*. Wants are a whole other topic!)

When I think about faith and a bunch of folks who had every reason to worry, I really don't have to go any further than the Hall of Fame of biblical heroes in Hebrews 11. First, in that chapter, faith is defined: "Now faith is the reality of what is hoped for, the proof of what is not seen. For our ancestors won God's approval by it" (vv. 1-2). Then after briefly speaking about creation, the writer (we are not sure who wrote this great epistle) launches into a laundry list of heroes, a solid group of folks who, had they spent their time worrying, would likely not have been in such favor with God.

I love this entire chapter, but verse 8 is my favorite: "By faith Abraham, when he was called, obeyed and went out to a place he was going to receive as an inheritance. He went out, not knowing where he was going." How many times have we asked God to tell us right now where we are going and when? Or told God what we intend to do rather than share our concerns with Him and let Him direct us at the right time to the answer? I am so guilty of telling God what to do rather than waiting on Him.

Philippians 4:6 also addresses worry: "Don't worry about anything, but in everything, through prayer and petition with thanksgiving, let your requests be made known to God." We must have the kind of relationship with God that requires an investment of time and a setting aside of the mess of the world (the stuff you worry about) as we come to know Him better. Worrywarting gets you nothing but ulcers and frustration. God meets needs, fulfills promises, and even saves folks from themselves. His timing may not be what we would desire, and His answers may not be what we want, but His timing is exactly right, and His answers bring Him glory. Trust Him. Place your worries in His capable hands.

prayer

Lord, I confess to You that I worry about stuff. Help me commit my hopes, dreams, and needs to You. Guard my heart and prepare my mind for Your answers. Show me what is important and help me to leave the other things behind. Help me to be found faithful. Amen.

What Next?

Study Hebrews 11. List the heroes and what they accepted on faith.

Look at your prayer journal—are the requests in it truly "desires of your heart" or just stuff you have decided you need or want?

Day 31

Out of the Slimy Pit

> *I waited patiently for the LORD, and He turned to me and heard my cry for help. He brought me up from a desolate pit, out of the muddy clay, and set my feet on a rock, making my steps secure. He put a new song in my mouth, a hymn of praise to our God. Many will see and fear and put their trust in the LORD.*
>
> *—Psalm 40:1-3*

Harold, the local town drunk, often cut through the cemetery on the outskirts of town as he wandered home after a night of excessive drinking. On this unusually dark evening, however, things took an unexpected turn. Unaware a new grave had been dug, an inebriated Harold stumbled headfirst into the hole. For what seemed like hours, he struggled to get out of the seven-foot-deep hole. He tried jumping, climbing, and even getting a running start to try and propel himself from the pit. Nothing worked. Harold finally resigned himself to the fact he was stuck, so he retreated to the corner of the grave and settled down for the night. An hour or so later, a local farmer was out on his nightly coon hunt and, against his better judgment, decided to take a shortcut through the cemetery. As he walked rapidly across the dimly lit graveyard he also managed to fall into the open hole. In a state of panic, the farmer began desperately trying to get out . . . completely unaware that Harold sat in the darkness at the other end of the grave. For several minutes Harold watched the farmer clawing and climbing as he tried to ascend the sides of the grave, then he reached over in darkness, laid a hand on the farmer's shoulder, and said, "Just give up. You can't get out of here." *But that farmer did!*

If you live long enough you'll find yourself in a pit—not a pleasant place to be. The pit is often dark, cold, and lonely. And like Harold and the old farmer, we claw, climb, and jump trying to pull ourselves out. Many times it's simply no use. In these moments all we can do is

78

wait. This is the lesson David is teaching us in Psalm 40:1, "I waited patiently for the LORD, and He turned to me and heard my cry for help." David may have been stuck in a pit . . . sinking in the mud . . . waiting . . . but he continued to worship.

But waiting is hard. In fact for many, waiting feels a lot like doing nothing. In a world that admires aggressiveness, waiting can make us feel lethargic, ineffective, and complacent. Waiting for the Lord, however, is none of these things. Patiently waiting for the Lord is about expectancy, not despair. We look forward to what God will do . . . and we wait for Him to act in His time. As Solomon remind us, "He has made everything appropriate in its time. He has also put eternity in their hearts, but man cannot discover the work God has done from beginning to end" (Ecclesiastes 3:11).

God pulled David from the pit and put a new song in his mouth and a hymn of praise in his heart. Worship sustains us in the pit and allows us to celebrate once we are out!

prayer

Father, I confess that being in the pit is hard. Today I cry out asking for patience while waiting for You to work in Your time. Allow my worship to be ceaseless, even though Your plans may be unclear. May songs of praise to You define this period of my life. In Jesus' name, amen.

What Next?

Reflect on a time you found yourself in a pit. Why was waiting so difficult? What is the main lesson from Psalm 40 you can apply to your life today?

Day 32

Invisible People

Happy is one who cares for the poor; the LORD will save him in a day of adversity.

—Psalm 41:1

That guy at the intersection with the sign is very real. So is the lady and her young child bedding down using a cardboard box under the bridge. But somehow if I look away and avoid eye contact, then it's like they're not there. In a psychological illusion even Houdini would applaud, I'm able to make them disappear. It's as though they are invisible or, even better, don't exist at all. These invisible people populate our cities and communities . . . undetected by the vast majority. Why? The answer is simple: when we come face to face with poverty, especially homelessness, it's much easier to look away.

On a single night in January 2015, 564,708 people slept outside, in an emergency shelter, or in transitional housing. In 2015, 17.7 people in every 10,000 were homeless across the USA. In Mississippi where I live, it was 7 in every 10,000. This is unacceptable in a nation where the average worker spends nearly $1,100 a year on coffee.

Our worship ministry intentionally partners with organizations to combat homelessness and poverty. We've performed benefit concerts for the Nashville Rescue Mission and worked in shelters in major cities like Dallas, New York, San Diego, and Miami. Our church has numerous ministries for the poor, including legal, medical, and dental care, and buys school supplies, clothing, and Christmas presents for children whose parents are incarcerated. Even with all this . . . I can still make them disappear:

> At the traffic light where a man holds a "Will Work for Food" sign . . . I look away.

> At the gas station where a man and wife sit outside in freezing temperatures . . . I look away.

On the side of the street as a woman pushes a grocery cart
. . . I look away.

At a checkout line as a hungry child watches her mom count
pennies . . . I look away.

In Psalm 41, David encourages us to open our eyes and our hearts
to the poor. It's the principle of sowing and reaping. If we become
God's hands and feet for those in need, He will "save us in our day of
adversity." Jesus addressed this in Matthew 25:40–43:

> *And the King will answer them, "I assure you: Whatever*
> *you did for one of the least of these brothers of Mine, you*
> *did for Me." Then He will also say to those on the left,*
> *"Depart from Me, you who are cursed, into the eternal*
> *fire prepared for the Devil and his angels! For I was hun-*
> *gry and you gave Me nothing to eat; I was thirsty and*
> *you gave Me nothing to drink; I was a stranger and you*
> *didn't take Me in; I was naked and you didn't clothe Me,*
> *sick and in prison and you didn't take care of Me."*

Will you open your eyes to the poverty around you? If you do, it will
change the way you live.

prayer

Dear Father, I confess that too many times I look away from
those in need. Convict me to look into their faces and sense
their hopelessness. I ask that You help me be a blessing to
the poor and that my own selfishness be broken in order to
help others. Amen.

What Next?

Take time today to intentionally notice the people in need around
you. Look into their faces and sense the pain in their lives. Do one
thing today to bring hope to someone's life.

Day 33

Are You Thirsty?

As a deer longs for streams of water, so I long for You, God. I thirst for God, the living God.

—*Psalm 42:1-2*

If you ever travel to Israel, a must-see destination is Masada. It was here, atop this mountain in the Judean desert and overlooking the Dead Sea, that Herod the Great built a luxurious fortress. It was also here where Jewish rebels bravely fought the Romans in the siege of Masada, eventually committing mass suicide in AD 74 when defeat was imminent.

Several years ago our worship ministry visited this site during a missions trip to the Holy Land. In addition to the excavated Roman camp site, bath houses, palace remains, and synagogue, one of the highlights of the trip, for those brave enough to try it, was descending from the summit on the Snake Path, a winding 2.5-mile downward trail that drops more than 1,300 feet from the top and took us almost an hour to navigate. Because our trip was in mid-July, the temperature that day was well above 100 degrees. Halfway down, the intensity of the heat began to take its toll on all of us. As we paused to take a break, I reached into my backpack for a bottle of water to try and quench my thirst. To my dismay, the water in the bottle was too hot to drink. Needless to say, once we reached the base of the path, the first thing each of us did was buy multiple bottles of cold water.

Just as physical thirst leaves us craving for water, our parched souls can only be satisfied by communion with God. That's what the psalmist is saying, "I thirst for God, the living God." Are you suffering from spiritual thirst? If so, why?

One of the primary reasons for a dry spirit is not gathering with fellow believers for worship. Recent research shows that more than 80 percent of Americans do not regularly attend church and between 4,000 and 7,000 churches close their doors each year.

And let us be concerned about one another in order to promote love and good works, not staying away from our worship meetings, as some habitually do, but encouraging each other, and all the more as you see the day drawing near.

—*Hebrews 10:24-25*

A second symptom of spiritual thirst is not spending time alone with God on a consistent basis. If you are experiencing spiritual dehydration, how long has it been since you've earnestly sought His presence by spending time in Scripture? How's your prayer life? Is your life so busy that God has been displaced? Have your blocked God out due to life's circumstances?

prayer

Dear Lord, I confess my spirit is barren and dry. Like the deer quarantined from water, my soul is on the verge of collapse. Please quench my thirsty heart with Your sweet presence. Amen.

What Next?

Do you remember a time you were physically thirsty? How did you feel? Take five minutes to honestly evaluate your personal walk with God.

How's your Bible study?

Is your prayer life consistent and growing?

Identify three specific things you can do to protect your personal time with God . . . and do them.

Day 34

Wake Up, Lord!

Wake up, LORD! Why are You sleeping? Get up! Don't reject us forever! Why do You hide Yourself and forget our affliction and oppression?

—Psalm 44:23-24

Near midnight on April 14, 1912, the RMS *Titanic* struck an iceberg on its maiden voyage from Southampton to New York City. Two hours and forty minutes later the largest passenger liner in the world at the time had sunk to the bottom of the North Atlantic Ocean, resulting in one of the most infamous disasters in maritime history.

Six-year-old Douglas Spedden slept through the initial collision and only briefly woke when he was taken to a lifeboat. Within minutes he was back asleep and managed to remain so throughout the night in spite of the chaos around him. When he woke the next morning and saw the icebergs all around he said, "Look at the beautiful North Pole with no Santa Claus on it!"

Do you ever feel as though God is sleeping through the chaos of your life? Are you going through a difficult time and feel that God is far away from you? David experienced this, also. All around him, evil seemed to triumph and injustice appeared to go unpunished. In response, David cried out in verse 23, "Wake up, LORD! Why are you sleeping?"

If we're honest, when we see injustice or evil go seemingly unpunished, it makes us angry. How can God allow this? Why won't He do something? In these moments, our ability to authentically worship can become impaired as we try to take matters into our own hands. Take it from experience—that never works! In Psalm 121:4, the psalmist reminds us that the God who protects us never sleeps or slumbers. That's a promise that can help us take rest in the midst of the chaos of our lives.

prayer

All-seeing God, forgive me for not trusting You in times of uncertainty and despair. Today, when I look around and see evil abounding, give me the peace and comfort that comes from knowing You are in control. Allow me to live out a godly confidence that will be seen by those around me so that You will be glorified. In the precious name of Jesus Christ, amen.

What Next?

What areas of your life have created stress points in your walk with God? Is there injustice or evil around you that has been ignored? Make a list of these things, and intentionally place them under the authority of a God who never sleeps!

Day 35

Here Comes the Bride

*Your throne, God, is forever and ever; the scepter of Your
kingdom is a scepter of justice. You love righteousness and
hate wickedness; therefore God, your God, has anointed
you with the oil of joy more than your companions.*

—Psalm 45:6–7

As a father of daughters, I knew the day would come. The
long-dreaded phone call, followed by the lunch meeting
where you sit across the table from this suitor, awkwardly
picking at your food and skirting the main topic, until finally he
blurts out: "I'd like to ask your daughter to marry me." On the
inside I scream at the top of my lungs, "Nooooo!" On the outside I
smile and say all the right things. Truth is, for years this day has
been inevitable. As I look at the young, good-looking guy staring
back at me, he knows my options are limited. My daughter loves
him. He wins the day . . . and he knows it!

For me, this scene played out twice in painfully close succession.
The result: two weddings within ten months. Because of our love
of Disney, small weddings were not even on the radar. Both older
daughters, Kayla and Lizzie, were convinced they were inadvertently dropped off at our house instead of Cinderella's castle after
they were born. So with visions of fairy tales and "Happily Ever
After" endings in mind, the wedding planning commenced.

To be honest, those weddings were pretty amazing events in our
lives. Friends and family joined us in the celebration. There was
food, music, dancing. Heck, by the end of the reception, I had even
grown to like the men with whom my daughters had chosen to share
life. It was a beautiful transition to a new chapter.

Psalm 45, described as "A Royal Wedding Song," is a poetic love
song detailing the romance between a bride and groom on their wedding day. "My heart is moved by a noble theme as I recite my verses
to the king; my tongue is the pen of a skillful writer" (v. 1).

While this wedding song was written for one of the kings of Israel, possibly Solomon or Ahab, it has a second, more critical meaning. The author of Hebrews reveals that Psalm 45 is a Messianic psalm referring to Jesus: "Your throne, God, is forever and ever, and the scepter of Your kingdom is a scepter of justice" (Hebrews 1:8). But who is Christ's bride? Paul reveals in 2 Corinthians 11:2, "For I am jealous over you with a godly jealousy, because I have promised you in marriage to one husband—to present a pure virgin to Christ." This means that as Christians, we are the betrothed of Christ. Psalm 45 is a love song between Christ and His church.

A love relationship with Christ? Now that's what worship was intended to be!

prayer

Lord Jesus, You are our beautiful King, and we long for You like a bride longs for her husband. I pray that You protect me with purity so that I can be worthy. Cleanse me, Father. Amen.

What Next?

In your own words write a paragraph describing what it means to be the fiancée of Christ. What are the practical implications of this in relation to worship?

Day 36

Always Near

God is our refuge and strength, a helper who is always found in times of trouble.

—Psalm 46:1

Several years ago, I heard a story about an old Wyoming rancher who was out checking his fence on the backside of his farm. Driving across the rocky terrain he lost control of his trusty pickup truck and plummeted off a cliff. Facing an imminent death, he jumped from the truck on the way down and grabbed a branch growing out of the cliff. After hanging there for what seemed an eternity, in desperation he yelled, "Is anybody up there?" After a moment of silence, a voice rang out: "Son, this is God. Have faith and let go of the branch." The old rancher looked down on the rocky ravine and cried out, "Is anybody else up there?"

Faith is having complete trust or confidence in something or someone. Have you ever had your faith shattered? Maybe you trusted someone who let you down—an abusive parent, a respected leader, a spouse who was unfaithful. Maybe your faith was shaken in response to the failure of a trusted institution such as a bank, university, or even a church.

The harsh reality is that people make mistakes. Leaders fail. Banks close. Churches lose focus. When our faith is based on what is temporary, we end up disillusioned, skeptical, and filled with uncertainty. By contrast, when our commitment is in the Rock of Ages, we cannot be shaken.

Joshua needed to hear this. Moses was dead, but God was about to deliver on the Promise He made some 40 years earlier. The Promised Land was in sight. Great obstacles, however, lay ahead: the fortified city of Jericho, the city of Ai, battles with the Hittites, Amorites, Canaanites, Perizzites, Hivites, and Jebusites. For Joshua to claim God's promise, he needed an unwavering faith.

The same is true for us. In a world saturated with hopelessness and despair, our path to victory seems riddled with obstacle after obstacle. Sometimes it seems the battles are simply too great. That's where faith steps in.

prayer

Lord, speak to me today for I am listening. I come before you with a heart of worship. Give me the peace to rest on Your promise to never leave me, and grant me, like Joshua, an unwavering faith. Amen.

What Next?

Take time to meditate on Psalm 136. This Psalm of David, a hymn, was sung in Solomon's Temple (2 Chronicles 7:3, 6) and by the armies of Jehoshaphat as they marched to battle in the wilderness of Tekoa. Written in a call-and-response format, the phrase, "His love is eternal," appears in each of the 26 verses. After experiencing this great hymn, you can claim God's promise to never leave us. His love is eternal!

$\mathcal{D}ay$ 37

Applause?

Clap your hands, all you peoples; shout to God with a jubilant cry. For Yahweh, the Most High, is awe-inspiring, a great King over all the earth.

—Psalm 47:1-2

While in seminary, chapel services were a little stuffy. However, one chapel service I remember took stuffy to an entirely new level. As the music professor approached the pulpit area, he did so as a man on mission. "In a few minutes," he said, "our soloist will come and lead us in worship. Let's give him a round of applause." The seminarians responded enthusiastically. Now, those who knew the professor were aware he opposed clapping during worship services. We were intrigued, yet perplexed. He continued, "Next week our seminary choir will be leading in worship. Let's give them a round of applause." Again, those in attendance obliged. This sequence continued, back and forth, with the level of applause consistently declining in proportion with a growing suspicion that something wasn't right. Finally, the professor said, "That covers all our guests for the semester. There should be no further applause from this point forward." Of course, this had zero impact on the 1,000 or so seminary students. If anything, they began to applaud everything. Even the guy giving announcements started getting thunderous applause! The professor was livid. The students felt vindicated. Nothing was resolved.

The question of the appropriateness of applause in worship has created tension for decades. In the late 1990s, I decided to write an article for our church paper to answer the question once and for all. Bad move. Now everyone was mad! Those who supported clapping felt I stifled their worship and set the church back decades. Those opposing applause believed I had opened the gates of hell and turned our services into rock concerts. At the risk of reliving that nightmare, here are a few thoughts:

First, clapping is biblical expression of worship. Psalm 47 makes this clear.

Second, applause as an act of worship must be directed to God, not individuals. Sometimes I wonder whom we honor in our worship services. Are we applauding the quality of the presentation? Are we honoring the soloists, choir, or musicians? Are we celebrating the song's message or its messenger? While saying thank you for an excellent presentation isn't inherently bad, as worshippers, our responses must first and foremost be directed to God. Misdirected applause undergirds a performance-driven worship model that displaces God as the central focus of worship. This is unacceptable and borders on idolatry.

Third, everything doesn't prompt applause. There are times when the only response is to exuberantly clap our hands in response to the greatness of God. Other times we can be so overcome with His mercy and grace the only appropriate response is a deafening silence. As worshippers we must pray for discernment to know the difference.

prayer

Father, may our worship be directed to You, an audience of one. I pray for discernment as to how I should respond in worship and for a heart that allows me to direct my response in the right direction. Protect my heart from seeking the applause of men. Amen.

What Next?

Intentionally think through how you respond in worship. To whom is your applause directed?

How long has it been since you applauded God for who He is?

Day 38

A Clean Heart

God, create a clean heart for me and renew a steadfast spirit within me.

—*Psalm 51:10*

In July 1985, 69-year-old violinist Julian Altman, dying from cancer, tried one more time to play his beloved violin. He managed three measures but was too weak to continue. He handed the violin to his wife Marcelle Hall and asked her to take care of it. Once home, Hall discovered several old newspaper articles in the violin's case. They covered the mysterious disappearance of a Stradivarius violin. The missing instrument, made in 1713 in the Cremona, Italy, workshop of Antonio Stradivari, history's greatest violin maker, was among the finest in the world and had been stolen in 1936 from the Carnegie Hall dressing room of Polish virtuoso Bronislaw Huberman.

Hall returned to the hospital and asked the dying Altman if his violin was the missing Stradivarius. Altman nodded. He'd had a troubled life, even spending time in prison, never able to claim the stolen violin or reap the benefits of owning a Stradivarius. Two years later, Hall returned the violin to Lloyds of London in exchange for a $263,000 finder's fee. The violin is now owned by violinist Joshua Bell who paid nearly $4 million for the instrument.

While not a great man, Altman reminds us of the enormous weight of our sin in our lives. When unconfessed it leaves us restless and unsettled, the sin blocking us from intimacy with God. Such was the case with David.

R. C. Sproul wrote, "The greatest fall of one of the church's most beloved saints brought forth one of the most cherished psalms in the Scriptures." Psalm 51, which is filled with gut-wrenching emotion, was written in response to Nathan's confrontation of David's affair with Bathsheba. As we read the verses of Psalm 51, we find David brokenhearted before God. His plea for mercy comes from the innermost depths of his soul. Not only did David confess his sin, he begged God to restore their relationship: "God, create a clean heart for me and renew a steadfast spirit within me. Do not banish me from Your presence or take Your Holy Spirit from me. Restore the joy of Your salvation to me, and give me a willing spirit" (Psalm 51:10–12).

Sin forms a barrier between us and God, blocking our ability to communicate with Him. Worship ceases as a result of this broken relationship. That's why David prays in verse 7: "Purify me with hyssop, and I will be clean; wash me, and I will be whiter than snow." Through forgiveness the broken relationship is restored. And with forgiveness, worship returns to the life of the believer: "If we confess our sins, He is faithful and righteous to forgive us our sins and to cleanse us from all unrighteousness" (1 John 1:9).

prayer

Father, I confess my life is plagued by sin. I ask You make me fully aware of sinful thoughts, words, or deeds so I might experience the joy of Your forgiveness. In the powerful name of Jesus, amen.

What Next?

Take a few minutes to reflect on your prayer life. How intentional are you in confessing sin in your life?

Paraphrase Psalm 51 in your own words, and pray it each day this week.

Day 39

Choose Your Epitaph

Here is the man who would not make God his refuge, but trusted in the abundance of his riches, taking refuge in his destructive behavior. But I am like a flourishing olive tree in the house of God; I trust in God's faithful love forever and ever.

—Psalm 52:7–8

Famous Epitaphs

A tomb now suffices him for whom the world was not enough. —Alexander the Great

There goes the neighborhood. —Rodney Dangerfield, actor

That's all, folks! —Mel Blanc, Warner Bros. voice actor

Free at last. Free at last. Thank God Almighty I'm Free At Last. —Martin Luther King Jr.

How will you be remembered after you die? What will your obituary contain? What will be said at your funeral? What will be your epitaph?

David penned Psalm 52 as he ran from Saul. It is a tale of two men, one evil and the other God-fearing. The evil man takes "refuge in his destructive behavior," while the man who fears God is like "a flourishing olive tree in the house of God." In truth, all of us were at some point like the evil man, but through the saving grace of Jesus Christ, our lives can be miraculously transformed into something beautiful in His sight.

If you have an opportunity to visit the Billy Graham Library in Charlotte, North Carolina, it's well worth the time. The 40,000-square-foot museum traces the life and ministry of Graham from his childhood days growing up on a dairy farm through his worldwide crusade ministry preaching to more than 2.2 billion people. One of my favorite epitaphs belongs to Graham's wife Ruth, who died in 2007 and is buried onsite in the Prayer Garden. This simple yet profound statement pretty much sums up our walk as believers in Christ:

End of Construction—Thank you for your patience.

prayer

Father, thank You for saving me from my sinful ways and guiding me on the path of righteousness. Allow me to be planted in the center of Your will and for my life to flourish as I seek Your face. Shape my life so that I will leave a legacy of faith and commitment to those who come after me. Amen.

What Next?

Take a few minutes to reflect on what your epitaph would say if written today. Compare that with what you want it to say. What are things you can do to shape the legacy you will one day leave?

Day 40

Do You Need a Redo?

*God looks down from heaven on the human race to see if
there is one who is wise, one who seeks God.*

—Psalm 53:2

As a sports official for many years, I've worked many big games across multiple sports. It didn't start that way. As most rookie football officials do, I gained my early gridiron experience working Saturday peewee games. Youth football is a virtual laboratory for would-be referees because most anything can happen . . . and usually does! Though often calm, these games can get brutal at time with coaches yelling and screaming as the young "super stars" live out the elusive dreams of their parents. During my second year, I somehow managed to be the senior official on the field for a cross-town rivalry football game. This meant I got to wear the white hat and serve as head referee. As officials, we were still in training, struggling with the rules and making correct calls. Even so, except for a few missed holding calls, the first half went smoothly . . . but that all changed after halftime.

At kickoff, the ball descended into a pile of converging nine- and ten-year-old boys, a pile defined by one common characteristic: mass chaos. There was no offense or defense, no visitor or home. As the ball disappeared into the pile there was only one goal: survival. Helmets flew, hair was pulled, people were screaming, all while the growing pile of childhood humanity grew taller and taller. There was genuine concern someone might be crushed. In an effort to prevent injury, one of the officials blew the whistle. Now to be honest, I have no clue who it was . . . no one ever admitted to it. Here's why. As the final strains of the whistle sounded, we realized a young kid from the receiving team had somehow escaped the pile undetected and was now standing in the end zone with the football. What should have been a touchdown was now an inadvertent whistle, the football official's worst nightmare.

In the midst of such a rule malady, confusion reigned supreme. After a lengthy discussion at midfield, I called the coaches together and said, "Guys, we ain't got a clue what to do." The only redeeming factor was they didn't either. Then someone made the greatest suggestion ever—act like it never happened and rekick. Believe it or not, everyone agreed, so we started over. We had been given a do-over.

If you remember our time together on Day 11, then Psalm 53 probably sounds familiar. That's because Psalm 53 is nearly identical to Psalm 14. Written by David, Psalm 14 celebrates the crossing of the Red Sea while Psalm 53, written nearly 300 years after David died, deals with the Israelite's salvation from the Assyrians. In essence, Psalm 53 is a do-over of Psalm 14, allowing a later event to be celebrated with much the same wording. This approach is similar to a new verse being added to an old hymn we've sung for years. It's the same old song, just given an additional verse.

prayer

God of second chances, thank You for allowing me the opportunity on occasion to get a do-over in life. Use my experiences to prevent me from repeating mistakes. Shape me through life's hardest experiences. In the name of Jesus, Amen.

What Next?

Reflect on a time in your life when God gave you a second chance. What did you learn from the experience? How did it shape your walk with Him?

Day 41

A Real Relationship

God, save me by Your name, and vindicate me by Your might! God, hear my prayer; listen to the words of my mouth. For strangers rise up against me, and violent men seek my life. They have no regard for God.

—Psalm 54:1–3

Far too often we as worshippers live our lives going through the motions: attending church, being active in small groups, singing at the top of our lungs in worship. At the end of the day, though, it's all a façade. The relationship simply doesn't exist.

It reminds me of the wife who longed to hear her husband say he loved her. His response? "Honey, I told you I loved you when we got married; if I ever change my mind, I'll let you know." An intimate and growing relationship is dependent upon spending time together and consistently communicating. Think about it. Have you ever had a close friend with whom you never talked? No. It's also unfathomable to think a close relationship with God is possible without spending time and communicating with Him. The psalmist understood a vibrant prayer life that binds our hearts to His is indispensable.

As worshippers, how often have we neglected our private relationship with the Father only to put on our nice clothes, stroll into corporate worship, and do and say all the right things, all while hiding that we are at a point of spiritual bankruptcy? There is no real relationship. It's like the couple who to the world looks like they have everything together only to one day announce they are getting a divorce. From the outside, everything looked great, but the marriage rotted from the inside long ago. In Luke 18, Jesus warned the Pharisees about false piety:

Two men went up to the temple complex to pray, one a Pharisee and the other a tax collector. The Pharisee took his stand and was praying like this: "God, I thank You that

I'm not like other people—greedy, unrighteous, adulterers,
or even like this tax collector. I fast twice a week; I give
a tenth of everything I get." But the tax collector, stand-
ing far off, would not even raise his eyes to heaven but
kept striking his chest and saying, "God, turn Your wrath
from me —a sinner!" I tell you, this one went down to his
house justified rather than the other; because everyone who
exalts himself will be humbled, but the one who humbles
himself will be exalted.

—vv.10-14

God knows the status of our relationship with Him. Going through
the motions doesn't fool Him, and we pay the price with a cold, powerless spiritual life.

prayer

Lord Jesus, thank You for the gift of prayer. I confess that
at times drawing close to You is not a priority and that as
a worshipper I lose my power source. Help me protect my
time with You each day and to listen to what You have to say
to me. In the name of Jesus, amen.

What Next?

Take a few minutes to evaluate your prayer life. Do you have a consistent time to pray? Are you keeping a journal to record how God
speaks to you, as well as to record answered prayers? Make a commitment to spend 15 minutes today seeking Him in prayer.

Day 42

"Et tu, Brute?"

*Now it is not an enemy who insults me—otherwise I could
bear it; it is not a foe who rises up against me—otherwise I
could hide from him. But it is you, a man who is my peer,
my companion and good friend!*

—Psalm 55:12-13

I love history. I prefer biographies over fiction, museums over
theme parks (except Disney World), and presidential libraries
over going to the movies. History informs us and can teach us
if we allow it.

One of the greatest figures in history was Julius Caesar of the
Roman Empire, who was assassinated in 44 BC. The conspiracy to
murder Caesar included a many as 60 senators, including his friend,
Marcus Brutus. In William Shakespeare's play (*Julius Caesar*, 1599)
Caesar recognizes his friend among the assassins and famously
utters the words, *"Et tu, Brute?"* meaning "And you, Brutus?"

Have you ever been betrayed by someone close to you? If so, you
understand the depth of hurt that results from that experience.
David was in great distress when he wrote Psalm 55. Although not
clear from the text, many scholars believe the psalm was written in
response to the rebellion of his son, Absalom. This certainly would
explain David's deep pain in verse 12, "Now it is not an enemy who
insults me—otherwise I could bear it."

Betrayal comes in many forms: gossip, broken confidence, failure
to stand in the gap during a difficult time, harsh criticism. When
these things come our way, that old backstabbing feeling is hard to
overcome. Our faith and confidence in the Lord, however, can help us
move forward. David realized that, writing in verse 22, "Cast your
burden on the LORD, and He will sustain you; He will never allow
the righteous to be shaken."

How should we respond? While there certainly will be negative emotions, we must embrace a spirit of forgiveness. The Greek word for forgiveness literally means to "let go." While very hard to do, it is necessary for us to move beyond betrayal. Jesus reminded us our worship is in vain with unforgiveness and broken relationships in our lives:

> *So if you are offering your gift on the altar, and there you remember that your brother has something against you, leave your gift there in front of the altar. First go and be reconciled with your brother, and then come and offer your gift.*
>
> *—Matthew 5:23-24*

We only hurt ourselves when we cling to bitterness and hatred. Embrace forgiveness today.

prayer

Father, help me model my life after You and to let go of the hurts that have come my way. Create in me a heart that is open to forgiveness and restoration, and allow me to move beyond my hurt. Amen.

What Next?

Make a list of people who've offended you. Are you holding grudges? Are these relationships still broken?

Read Luke 22. How did Jesus respond to betrayal in His life? What can you learn from this?

Day 43

The Great Escape

LORD, look! They set an ambush for me. Powerful men attack me, but not because of any sin or rebellion of mine. For no fault of mine, they run and take up a position. Awake to help me, and take notice.

—Psalm 59:3-4

Tower of London (1597)—Jesuit priest John Gerard escaped certain execution for promoting his Catholic beliefs during the reign of Queen Elizabeth. Despite having his hands beaten and tortured as part of his punishment, during his escape from the Tower of London, Gerard descended on a rope strung from the tower to a boat berthed in the surrounding moat.

Libby Prison, Richmond, Virginia (1864)—In one of the most celebrated escapes of the American Civil War, 109 Union soldiers imprisoned in Virginia dug their way to freedom. Using chisels and wooden spittoons, a small group of officers worked for more than two weeks to dig a nearly 60-foot passageway out of the prison.

Auschwitz, Germany (1944)—Auschwitz was the largest Nazi concentration camp compound, consisting of three camps during World War II with more than 1 million prisoners executed. Two prisoners, Rudolph Vrba and Alfred Wetzler, hid in a woodpile for three nights, then, wearing stolen suits, they walked silently to their freedom. Once free, they helped expose the crimes committed at Auschwitz. Their accounts later became crucial to the prosecution of the Nazis.

People are fascinated with escape stories partly because they involve intrigue, suspense, and unexpected twists. Psalm 59, penned by David, was written in response to such an event. In 1 Samuel 19, Saul is under the influence of an evil spirit, having already tried to kill David with a spear. He doesn't stop there:

Saul sent agents to David's house to watch for him and kill him in the morning. But his wife Michal warned David, "If you don't escape tonight, you will be dead tomorrow!" So she lowered David from the window, and he fled and escaped. Then Michal took the household idol and put it on the bed, placed some goat hair on its head, and covered it with a garment. When Saul sent agents to seize David, Michal said, "He's sick." Saul sent the agents back to see David and said, "Bring him on his bed so I can kill him." When the messengers arrived, to their surprise, the household idol was on the bed with some goat hair on its head. Saul asked Michal, "Why did you deceive me like this? You sent my enemy away, and he has escaped!"

—vv. 11–17

Have you invited God into the battles of your life? Do you trust God to defend you when you cannot defend yourself? There is no enemy too strong for God to handle and no prison so strong to keep us captive. Through Jesus Christ we are free.

prayer

Lord, I confess my failure to rely on You when facing opposition. I ask You to defend me from those who would harm me. Encircle me with Your love, and comfort me with a freedom that only comes through You. Amen.

What Next?

What does Psalm 59 tell us about the way David faced the opposition of Saul?

What opposition are you facing in your life? List three things you can do to release the battle to God.

Day 44

I Will Not Be Shaken

He alone is my rock and my salvation, my stronghold; I will not be shaken.

—*Psalm 62:6*

We often sing Cliff Duren's arrangement of "I Will Not Be Shaken." That song has been around for a while, but I am not sure how it impacts our folks. Some probably think I schedule it because I am a fan of anything with an old-timey gospel feel to it. That may be part of it, but there is meat to this verse—in fact to this entire psalm. For one thing, we are singing pure Scripture. For another, it backs up how God holds us up and is that unshakeable foundation each of us needs.

Though it is not clear what was happening when David penned this psalm, tradition suggests it took place during the time of Absalom's rebellion. Seriously, try to imagine David's heartbreak over the sins of his children. David's son, Amnon, raped his sister, Tamar. Amnon was then killed by his brother, Absalom. Finally, Absalom was killed after rebelling against David and his kingdom. David was not in a good place emotionally. Plus, David was still dealing with the consequences of his own sins.

Still, David, the man after God's own heart, seeks peace and knows it can only be found in God.

I am at rest in God alone. —*Psalm 62:1*

He alone is my rock and my salvation. —*v. 2*

My hope comes from Him. —*v. 5*

He alone is my rock and my salvation. —*v. 6*

It is almost as though with every stanza he becomes stronger.

In Acts, we find Peter and John arrested for healing the sick and for preaching about Jesus' Resurrection in the Temple. When asked under whose authority they are doing these things, Peter, the rock Christ said He would build His church on, said:

> *This Jesus is the stone rejected by you builders, which has become the cornerstone. There is salvation in no one else, for there is no other name under heaven given to people, and we must be saved by it.*
>
> *—Acts 4:11–12*

David, Peter, John—standing on the Rock—*I will not be shaken!*

prayer

Lord, no matter the circumstances of my life, help me keep my feet firmly planted on the Rock of my salvation. Forgive my times of despair and doubt. Fill me with Your Spirit. Give me the courage to stand firm. Amen.

What Next?

Read Psalm 62, and list everything that only God can provide. Do you have the same foundation as David?

Read Acts 4:1–22, and list everything God provided to Peter and John. Contrast that with David in Psalm 62.

Day 45

Filling the Void

God, You are my God; I eagerly seek You. I thirst for You;
my body faints for You in a land that is dry, desolate,
and without water.

—Psalm 63:1

I t is in prayer that we bear the deepest parts of our soul. Our
dreams, fears, hurts, and deepest needs are laid before the
Father. Also, it is in these moments new life is breathed into
our worship. As we seek the face of God while allowing His presence to penetrate every recess of our being, our hearts are tuned to
His. What was once stale, ritualistic worship is transformed into
life-changing dialogue with the King of Glory.

George Müller understood the power of prayer. A legendary
prayer warrior, Müller ran a group of orphanages in England and
started 117 schools that provided education for more than 120,000
boys, most of them orphans. In 1877, Müller was traveling to Quebec, Canada, when his ship encountered a thick fog. Müller desperately needed to make his appointment in Quebec. An unsympathetic
captain explained they were slowing the ship for safety, and Müller
would simply have to miss his appointment. So Müller asked the captain if he could use the chartroom to pray for the fog to lift. Though
an unbeliever, the captain followed Müller to the chartroom and listened as Müller said a simple prayer. The captain began to pray too
but was stopped by Müller, partially for the captain's unbelief but
mainly because Müller believed his prayer to have been answered.
Müller led the captain back to the bridge, where they discovered
the fog lifted. Shortly thereafter, the captain professed his belief in
Müller's God.

We were created to have an intimate relationship with God. In
fact, every one of us has a longing deep with our being that can only
be filled by Him. We try to fill that emptiness with lots of things, but
nothing works. The void remains. One day Jesus met a Samaritan

woman trying to fill this void with many things other than God. But the more they talked, the more she craved the Living Water only Jesus could provide.

> *Jesus said, "Everyone who drinks from this water will get thirsty again. But whoever drinks from the water that I will give him will never get thirsty again—ever! In fact, the water I will give him will become a well of water springing up within him for eternal life."*
> —*John 4:13–14*

Are you thirsting for a deeper relationship with God? Has your worship become predictable and dry? Relentlessly pursue God through prayer and meditation, and when you do, your walk with Him will take on a new dimension.

prayer

Father, I confess my heart is restless and empty without Your ever-abiding presence. Allow me to cling to Your heart this day, and I beg You to shape my countenance to become like Yours. In the name of Jesus, I pray. Amen

What Next?

Is prayer a priority in your life?

What is one thing you can do today to improve your one-on-one time with God?

Day 46

Benediction

May God be gracious to us and bless us; look on us with favor . . . God will bless us, and all the ends of the earth will fear Him.

—*Psalm 67:1, 7*

I love a musical benediction. One of my favorites is known as the priestly blessing and the Aaronic benediction. This song comes entirely from Numbers 6:22–27 from Moses's blessing to Aaron. You have probably sung it too:

The Lord bless you and keep you,
The Lord lift His countenance upon you,
And give you peace, and give you peace,
The Lord make His face to shine upon you,
And be gracious unto you,
Be gracious. The Lord be gracious, gracious unto you,
Amen, Amen, Amen, Amen, Amen, Amen, Amen.

Though these days we seldom do the seven-fold amen, we do cling to the affirmation in this song. These same words and affirmation are found in Psalm 67:1. We want His favor—His mercy—His allowing us to remain though we are sinners who do not deserve it. Some of us need more mercy than others, but we all need it because we are all sinners. Charles Spurgeon said of this: "The best saints and the worst sinners may unite in this petition." We are all in need of this together.

And we push it further because we also want His blessing, for Him to be gracious to us. This is not a selfish "me, me, me" request. We are seeking His blessing so the world will know what He has done and come to salvation in Him.

Sandwiched between these verses is pure praise and thanksgiving—praises by His people and rejoicing of the nations for what God has done and continues to do. So very often, we (I) fail to thank Him and praise Him when He grants us mercy or when He blesses us. This psalmist does not make that mistake.

The word *benediction* can be defined as "the short blessing with which public worship is concluded." I wonder if the dictionary editors looked at Psalm 67, Numbers 6, and Ephesians 3:20 when they coined that definition?

> *Now to Him who is able to do above and beyond all that we ask or think according to the power that works in us—to Him be glory in the church and in Christ Jesus to all generations, forever and ever. Amen.*
>
> —*Ephesians 3:20*

prayer

Lord, thank You for Your mercy and for the blessings You surround me with—for provision, for health, for family, and most importantly, for my relationship with You. Lord, forgive me when I take You for granted. Amen.

What Next?

How do you close your personal worship time?

Look at other benedictions in the Bible. Study them for how you can better communicate with God as you seek His mercy and His blessing.

Day 47

Are You Connected to the Power Source?

Sing to God, you kingdoms of the earth; sing praise to the Lord, to Him who rides in the ancient, highest heavens. Look, He thunders with His powerful voice!
—Psalm 68:32–33

Worship serves as our lifeline to God. Without it we have no power. Worship is similar to the lamp on your table. When plugged in to the power source, a lamp gives off light and fulfills the functions for which it was created. When the flow of electricity is cut off, it cannot function as designed.

In order for us to love people as ourselves, which Jesus established as the second greatest commandment (Matthew 22:39), we must see them through the eyes and heart of our Lord by having a heart like His. That only happens when we connect to Him through worship. Churches struggling with low or nonexistent conversions, lack of passion for missions and evangelism, and weak commitment to ministry should look first at their passion for worship. The reason there is no power: we are not connected to the Power Source.

Several years ago I led a missions project to Chiang Mai, Thailand, where we visited a Buddhist temple on the outskirts of the city. As the team walked through the ornate structure, overlaid with gold and fine jewels and sitting high on a mountain, people were burning incense and bowing down before statues of Buddha. These people were sincere, energetic, and passionate—but the object of their worship had no power. It was an idol.

As Christians, we must aggressively pursue the power source. This means the passion of our lives must be the development of a love relationship with God through Jesus Christ. This is done first and foremost through our daily walk with Him in prayer, the study of His Word, and personal worship. Second, our corporate worship must become an overflow of our personal worship experiences where the primary focus is meeting with God. Third, our approach to worship must simply be a tool that allows us to experience the presence of God and grow in our relationship with Him. While our approach is important, it cannot be the primary focus of worship.

> *All authority has been given to Me in heaven and on earth. Go, therefore, and make disciples of all nations, baptizing them in the name of the Father and of the Son and of the Holy Spirit, teaching them to observe everything I have commanded you. And remember, I am with you always, to the end of the age.*
>
> *—Matthew 28:18–20*

> *But you will receive power when the Holy Spirit has come on you, and you will be My witnesses in Jerusalem, in all Judea and Samaria, and to the ends of the earth.*
>
> *—Acts 1:8*

prayer

All-powerful God, thank You for making Your power known to me through Your creation. I beg that my heart would be fettered to Yours and that my life would be perpetually empowered through You. I ask these things in the name of Your Son and my Savior, Jesus Christ. Amen.

What Next?

Write a prayer asking for God's power to be manifested in your life. What's a specific situation where you need God's power today?

Day 48

Experience and Wisdom

Don't discard me in my old age; as my strength fails, do not abandon me.

—Psalm 71:9

Over the past 30 years, the worship culture in the United States has experienced seismic shifts in what we do, how we do it, and the skill set required to pull it off each week. Beginning in the 1940s, church musicians were trained to be proficient in conducting, reading music, children's music, and student choirs. As churches embraced more contemporary forms of worship, however, the needed skills changed. Required musical proficiencies in piano, orchestras, and choirs were replaced with guitar, bands, and praise teams. Further complicating the situation, seminaries and Christian colleges charged with training church musicians simply ignored the worship shifts taking place, often chalking them up as trends or passing fads. The result was a generation of church musicians who lacked the basic skills required for success.

But hope was not lost.

Although classically trained, the vast majority of worship leaders viewed their calling through the prism of "ministers first and musicians second." Music was simply the tool used to engage the culture with the gospel. As a result, preferred methodologies took a back seat and most worship leaders chose to retool in order to be effective.

In other words . . . Choir guys learned to lead bands and vocal teams. Technologically illiterate ministers of music learned about in-ear monitoring, image magnification (IMAG), and environmental lighting. Pianists learned new approaches to music theory (i.e. Nashville Numbers). Worship pastors even traded in familiar composers and arrangers such as Bach and Tom Fettke for more recent folks, such as Bradley Knight.

But something happened . . . we grew older. Our hair turned gray, fell out, or, as in my case, both! While we listened to Chris Tomlin and Vertical Church Band, we also had Michael W. Smith, 4Him, and the Gaither Vocal Band on our playlists. And then *it* happened.

After tirelessly working to stay relevant . . . learning new skill sets . . . buying shirts that don't tuck in . . . we began to hear things like:

"Our people love you . . . but maybe it's time you move to an administrative roll."

"We love music . . . but our target doesn't sing in choirs."

"I know you have 35 players under the age of 30 . . . but the orchestra model doesn't work for us moving forward."

"Why do we have to sing hymns? They really don't speak to my generation."

"We love elder statesmen . . . just not on the platform."

So what do you do when one day you look up and your worship pastor has gotten older? Embrace the role he fills as part of your church family. You might be surprised how much his experience is needed.

prayer

Father, open my eyes to the contributions of all who touch my life. Thank You for the passion of the young and the wisdom of the mature, and allow me to cling to both. Amen.

What Next?

Examine your closest relationships. Are they demographically diverse or are they one-sided?

Make a list of six people of different ages who impact your life. Text or call them to say thank you.

$\mathcal{D}ay$ 49

Lord of the Seasons

The day is Yours, also the night; You established the moon and the sun. You set all the boundaries of the earth; You made summer and winter.

—Psalm 74:16–17

Growing up in Mississippi, we experienced two seasons: summer and football. In fact, the weather is so consistent, it's not unusual to wear shorts on Christmas Day or take a dip in the pool by mid-March. It was not until I was married and we lived in and traveled to different parts of the country that I experienced four distinct seasons.

While living in Lynchburg, Virginia, my family attended the National Cherry Blossom Festival in Washington, DC, an event that attracts 1.5 million people each spring. The event began in 1912 when Mayor Yukio Ozaki of Tokyo, Japan, gave 3,000 trees to the United States and has since become one of the most popular festivals in the country.

In the fall, one of our favorite places to visit is the Great Smoky Mountain National Park, the most-visited national park in the United States. Divided almost evenly between the states of North Carolina and Tennessee, more than 11.3 million people visited in 2016. Many coming for the seasonal foliage changes.

To experience winter, I visited a frozen Niagara Falls, which straddle the international border of the United States and Canada. During days of subzero temperatures, the rising mist from the falls freezes and creates a visual masterpiece. It truly is an amazing sight to behold.

Most of us look forward to the changing seasons when budding flowers signal the end of winter or trees take on hues of yellow and red as they usher in fall. Change, however, is not relegated to nature. Just as the seasons change, life can go from sunny to dark literally overnight. One minute the weather looks calm, the next it becomes stormy. Change in our lives is inevitable, and truthfully, its impact is generally out of our control.

The psalmist knew this. According to tradition, Psalm 74 addresses the destruction of the Temple by Nebuchadnezzar in 587 BC. The first 11 verses are emotionally devastating as Asaph recounts in graphic detail the manner in which God's dwelling was "utterly desecrated" (v. 7). Even though things seemed out of control, the psalmist reminds us that God "set all the boundaries of the earth" (v. 17). No matter how much turmoil we face, nor our season of life, the Lord is a constant presence.

prayer

Gracious and loving God, You are present with me through all seasons. Thank You for Your promise to never leave me or forsake me. Amen.

What Next?

Read Jeremiah 52, which details the fall of Jerusalem and the destruction of the Temple.

Now reread Psalm 74 in its entirety. What emotions are the psalmist experiencing?

What is the one lesson you can learn from Psalm 74?

Day 50

From Generation to Generation

We must not hide them from their children, but must tell a
future generation the praises of the LORD, His might, and
the wonderful works He has performed.

—Psalm 78:4

My grandfather was a larger-than-life figure in my life. Papa, as we called him, was in his midsixties when I was born and spent the next 30 years pouring into and shaping me. He taught me how to work, fish, and chew tobacco (I eventually gave up the latter). I never recall a time he wasn't there. Football, basketball, and baseball games? Present. Piano recitals, plays, and band concerts? Present.

Most importantly, from the day I was born, Papa taught me about Jesus. Some of my favorite memories are of him taking his large-print Bible and reading me the timeless stories from Scripture: the crossing of the Red Sea, Daniel and the lion's dean, Samson and Delilah, the prodigal son, Paul and Silas. But he didn't stop there. Papa showed me how to pray, taught me church attendance was not optional, and modeled a life of worship. Through storytelling, everything became his classroom.

When working in the garden, he taught me about commitment. "But Jesus said to him, 'No one who puts his hand to the plow and looks back is fit for the kingdom of God'" (Luke 9:62).

When dealing with conflict, he demonstrated forgiveness and restoration. "Be angry and do not sin. Don't let the sun go down on your anger" (Ephesians 4:26).

When helping someone less fortunate, he modeled compassion. "But a Samaritan on his journey came up to him, and when he saw the man, he had compassion" (Luke 10:33).

In a real sense, this is what is taking place in Psalm 78: faith in God is being passed from one generation to another. Over the course of 23 verses, God's work on behalf of His people is recounted. He reminds us of the faith of Abraham, Isaac, and Jacob. He remembers Moses, Joshua, Elijah, and King David. The psalmist is taking seriously the command of the *Shema* ("hear"), the most important prayer in Judaism:

> *Listen, Israel: The LORD our God, the LORD is One. Love the LORD your God with all your heart, with all your soul, and with all your strength. These words that I am giving you today are to be in your heart. Repeat them to your children. Talk about them when you sit in your house and when you walk along the road, when you lie down and when you get up. Bind them as a sign on your hand and let them be a symbol on your forehead. Write them on the doorposts of your house and on your gates.*
>
> *—Deuteronomy 6:4–9*

I'm very thankful that Papa took passing down his faith seriously. It made all the difference in who I am today.

prayer

Loving Father, thank You for the wondrous grace You've shown to me. Rise up in me a passion to share Your love and faithfulness with the next generation. Show me specific ways I can tell Your story to those around me. In Jesus' name. Amen.

What Next?

Take time today to tell the children in your life how you came to know Christ as your personal Savior.

Tell them how God has answered a specific prayer.

Day 51

There's No Place I'd Rather Be

Better a day in Your courts than a thousand anywhere else. I would rather be at the door of the house of my God than to live in the tents of wicked people.

—Psalm 84:10

My earliest memories of growing up in Mississippi revolve around Everett Baptist Church in rural Simpson County. Events like revival meetings, the annual Homecoming, and afternoon Stamps-Baxter singings punctuate the landscape of my childhood. The church building itself, complete with its white exterior, hardwood floors, and a Warner Sallman painting of the *Head of Christ* accenting the pulpit could have been used as a site location in *O Brother, Where Art Thou?* Outside, under a grove of oak trees, my uncles constructed wood tables that seemed to run the length of our high school football field. Those tables were used for regular dinner on the grounds and even held BBQ chicken plates for a benefit to raise money to help with medical expenses when my mom was diagnosed with throat cancer at the age of 25.

Attending church at Everett was a family experience. Each week three generations of uncles, aunts, and cousins—some 75 people total—would worship together. The songs came from *The Broadman Hymnal*, shape-note edition, and the preaching came from Brother Terry, a former junior college football player who loved the Lord with every fiber of his substantially overweight body. Brother Terry instilled in us a love for the Bible as the inerrant and infallible Word of God. His preaching could be summed up with three words: hard, long, and loud! Although the old building no longer stands, these images are pressed in my mind like a Polaroid photo from days long gone.

Enter my grandmother, Maggie Mae Thames, better known to us as Mama't. One of seven children, she was the matriarch of the entire family. Mama't called the shots. She was loud (Brother Terry nicknamed her Big Mouth . . . and she loved it) and the center of all gatherings. Her favorite hobby was talking, something she did incessantly. The thing that most defined her, however, was her love for her grandchildren. Because my mom was divorced with two small children by 17, Mama't stepped in as a constant presence in our lives. We probably spent more time at her house than our own. Mama't was the hub of our existence. And for her, church was as much a part of life as eating or sleeping. She embodied Psalm 84:10: "Better a day in Your courts than a thousand anywhere else." Skipping church was not an option, and suggesting it could have been detrimental to your health. I never even tried.

Mama't insisted we dress nicely for church, and when I started leading the singing at 15, she took great pride in making sure I had a "new" suit every year. If we couldn't find one in local garage sales, she would use her Gayfers charge card to buy me a Haggar machine-washable suit, the only time I ever saw her use credit. When she died a few years back at the age of 96, her greatest joy still was being with family and enjoying the things of God. The Apostle John's words really did define her, "I have no greater joy than this: to hear that my children are walking in the truth" (3 John 4). For Mama't, that was based first and foremost on a love for His church. That's a legacy I'm honored to receive!

prayer

Father, thank You for Your church and the power it has through You to change lives. Forgive me for the times I've failed to make it a priority in my life. Birth in me a fresh commitment to be faithful in my attendance in the house of the Lord. Amen.

What Next?

Evaluate your church attendance over the past six months. Is Psalm 84:10 a reality in your life?

Day 52

The Dark Enemy

*LORD, why do You reject me? Why do You hide Your face
from me?*

—Psalm 88:14

D epression is the dark enemy lurking beneath the surface of
too many lives . . . it's more common than you think. The
National Institute of Mental Health estimates 16 million
adults suffered at least one major depressive episode in the United
States in 2012. This doesn't include the 350 million people worldwide
who suffer from the illness. While the word *depression* is not specifically used in the Bible, its symptoms are clearly described.

Psalm 88, written by the Levite musician Heman the Ezrahite,
is possibly the saddest psalm in the Bible. Although Heman's faith
is implied in the opening verses, the remainder of the psalm takes
the reader on a dark journey punctuated with sadness and despair.
Even so, a sense of hope underscores the entire passage acknowledg-
ing Heman's worship in spite of his deep hurt.

Charles Haddon Spurgeon, known as the "Prince of Preachers,"
was no stranger to depression. By the age of 22, the young Spurgeon's ministry had risen to unprecedented success. A catastrophe
on the evening of October 19, 1856, however, forever changed his
life. His enormous popularity forced the rental of London's Surrey
Gardens Music Hall in order to accommodate the thousands who had
gathered to hear him preach that night. When someone in the crowd
shouted, "Fire!" panic spread. In the crowd's rush to escape, seven
people were trampled to death and several others seriously injured.
Spurgeon never fully recovered emotionally from the tragedy.

Even so, Spurgeon continued to share the gospel of Jesus for
another 35 years. On June 7, 1891, Spurgeon preached what would
be his last sermon.

*He is the most magnanimous of captains. There never was
his like among the choicest of princes. He is always to be*

found in the thickest part of the battle. When the wind blows cold he always takes the bleak side of the hill. The heaviest end of the cross lies ever on his shoulders. If he bids us carry a burden, he carries it also. If there is anything that is gracious, generous, kind, and tender, yea lavish and superabundant in love, you always find it in him. . . . His service is life, peace, joy. Oh, that you would enter on it at once! God help you to enlist under the banner of Jesus even this day. Amen.

When Spurgeon died in 1892, the world mourned. Mississippi native and founder of Southwestern Baptist Theological Seminary, B. H. Carroll noted, "If every crowned head in Europe had died that night, the event would not be so momentous as the death of this one man." More than 100,000 people lined the street as Spurgeon's coffin was moved to West Norwood Cemetery in London.

prayer

Father, help me, for I am battling the inner demons of depression, loneliness, and hopelessness. At this moment, I need Your strength and courage in my life. Allow me to find peace, happiness, and contentment in life. Amen.

What Next?

Read Psalm 88 and list different emotions experienced by the psalmist. Are there circumstances in your life causing you to be depressed? If so, how are you navigating this emotional journey? How is it impacting your worship?

Day 53

It All Belongs to Him

*The heavens are Yours; the earth also is Yours. The world
and everything in it—You founded them.*

—Psalm 89:11

A story is often told of a woman who finished her shopping and returned to her car to find four men inside it. She dropped her shopping bags, drew a handgun from her purse, and shouted at the men, "I have a gun, and I know how to use it! Get out of the car!" The men didn't stick around for a second invitation. They got out and ran like crazy! Understandably shaken, the woman quickly loaded her shopping bags and got into the car. She just wanted out of there as fast as possible, but, no matter how she tried, she couldn't get her key into the ignition. Then it hit her: *This isn't my car!*

She looked, and indeed her car was parked four or five spaces away. Realizing her mistake, she got out, loaded the bags into her own car, and drove to the police station to turn herself in. After hearing her story, the sergeant working the desk nearly fell out of his chair laughing. At the other end of the counter were four men reporting a carjacking by a woman with glasses and curly white hair, less than five feet tall, and carrying a large handgun. No charges were filed.

The woman thought it was her car, but it really belonged to someone else. The truth is: God owns everything, including that lady's car and the one she mistakenly entered. It all belongs to Him.

Charles Spurgeon called Psalm 89 the "Majestic Covenant Psalm" because it repeatedly refers to the covenant God initiated with David in 2 Samuel 7:1–17.

The LORD said, "I have made a covenant with My chosen one; I have sworn an oath to David My servant: 'I will establish your offspring forever and build up your throne for all generations.'"

—Psalm 89:3-4

The LORD declares to you: The LORD Himself will make a house for you. When your time comes and you rest with your fathers, I will raise up after you your descendant, who will come from your body, and I will establish his kingdom. He will build a house for My name, and I will establish the throne of his kingdom forever.

—2 Samuel 7:11-13

This messianic psalm, fulfilled in the person of Jesus Christ, is a 52-verse song of praise. It is undergirded with an unfaltering confidence that the God who owns it all has the power to keep His promises. David's lineage and throne will be protected. When we believe that God will keep His promises, our anxieties are drastically minimized. Take the pressure to fix everything off your shoulders and place it on God. Trust me, He can handle it!

prayer

Creator and Sustainer of the universe, I confess that at times my desire to control circumstances is great. Allow me to rely on Your strength, the One who owns it all, to direct my paths and act on my behalf. In the powerful name of Jesus. Amen.

What Next?

Read 2 Samuel 7:1-17.

Take a few minutes to list the promises found in Psalm 89.

Day 54

How Do I Count My Days?

Teach us to number our days carefully so that we may develop wisdom in our hearts.

—*Psalm 90:12*

A s a kid in Sunday School, we memorized Psalm 90:12. Honestly, I was always confused by it. How was I supposed to know how to count days? And if I could not count them, how in the world would I ever be wise? One thing for sure, we don't need to assume that our children understand the context when we give them a verse to memorize!

Psalm 90 is a song about life's dark side, about coming death. It is the only psalm attributed to Moses, thus the oldest psalm. Moses knew a lot about being a man without a country. He was saved by Pharaoh's daughter from the death promised Jewish baby boys. Later, when Pharaoh finally released the children of Israel, Moses became a fugitive of the only home he knew. Finally, because of his sin, he died before entering the Promised Land of Canaan, though God allowed him to see it from the distance. He also led a bunch of whining, complaining, doubting, sinning folks around in the desert for years because their faith was not sufficient even though God was with them day and night. Even so, Moses knew that the true dwelling place of man would not be a place; it was with God.

The early verses of chapter 90 talk about the frailty of man and the length of life lived in fear of God's wrath. Moses references things he wrote about in Genesis—the fall of man in the Garden of Eden, the flood, and that God's time is infinite while man's is limited. In verse 12, Moses prays for wisdom. We must know our limitations in this life and acknowledge our sin. Proverbs 9:10 reinforces it: "The fear of the LORD is the beginning of wisdom, and the knowledge of the Holy One is understanding." Acknowledgment of our sin leads to a changed heart, which leads to wisdom and prepares you to encounter God in worship.

The latter part of the Psalm 90 speaks of God's love and seeks His favor. The psalmist asks for relief—as much joy as there has been suffering. "Satisfy us in the morning with Your faithful love so that we may shout with joy and be glad all our days. Make us rejoice for as many days as You have humbled us, for as many years as we have seen adversity" (vv. 14-15). The psalmist wanted relationship with God. He wanted to worship.

prayer

Lord, I confess I am a whiner and a sinner. Make Your desires for me become my desires. Let my audience for worship not be myself but You. Amen

What Next?

Read Psalm 90 in its entirety. Note each Old Testament reference you find and how or if the sinner in each instance came back to God and worshipped.

Day 55

A Safe Place

I will say to the LORD, "My refuge and my fortress, my God, in whom I trust."

—Psalm 91:2

There are many psalms that talk about God being our refuge, rock, and fortress. Because of that, when we trust in Him we will not be shaken from our foundations. When I read Psalm 91, the song that comes to mind is "I Will Not Be Shaken" by Tommy Walker. In this song of worship, Walker expresses how God heard him crying for help and protected him from the enemy.

Some think the writer of the psalm could be Moses due to the similar structure of Psalm 90, but there is no evidence to confirm that. Nonetheless, it is rich. Jesus knew this psalm, as did Satan. Satan used it to test Jesus (Matthew 4:6; Luke 4:10–11) to have Him prove He was the Messiah. Jesus knew the deliverance described here, thus His confirmation as Messiah came with His death and resurrection.

Psalm 91:4 is a beautiful description of God as our refuge: "He will cover you with His feathers; you will take refuge under His wings. His faithfulness will be a protective shield."

One of our choir members has a refuge area for owls. Her photos are amazing. Over the years, the most moving pictures are those showing the mother owl wrapping her young in her feathers, protecting them from the elements and predators. That image comes alive for me in verse 4. Whatever terrors, wars, plagues, or pestilence surrounds me, I will rejoice in His protection of me! God protected me when He allowed Jesus to bear God's full wrath for my sin. And because He protects me, I will worship Him.

Likewise, the chorus and bridge of "I Will Not Be Shaken" really brings all of this back to faith in Him . . . God will not be moved, will never change, and will reign forever! He is our refuge and fortress for all times.

prayer

Lord, You are my rock, shield, and fortress, and I thank You for the security I have in You. Help me to never take it for granted. Keep my focus on You and away from the world. Amen.

What Next?

How has God protected you? Are you protected for eternity? Have you shared this news with others?

Day 56

Finishing Strong

The righteous thrive like a palm tree and grow like a cedar tree in Lebanon. Planted in the house of the LORD, they thrive in the courts of our God. They will still bear fruit in old age, healthy and green, to declare: "The LORD is just; He is my rock, and there is no unrighteousness in Him."
                                                                —Psalm 92:12–15

We live in a culture that often seems to undervalue age and experience. Even so, history is replete with success stories accomplished by people over the age of 50:

Grandma Moses didn't start painting until she was in her seventies.

Colonel Harland Sanders was in his sixties when he began his Kentucky Fried Chicken empire.

Laura Ingalls Wilder published her *Little House on the Prairie* series when she was in her sixties.

Throughout the Bible we see examples of mature godly leaders accomplishing amazing things:

Near the end of his life, **Isaac** passed along a prophetic blessing that continues to impact the world today.

At 130 years old, **Jacob** moved his entire family to Egypt and passed along a blessing to his children and grandchildren.

Moses led the Israelites until the age of 120, and **Caleb** led the charge into the Promised Land at the age of 85.

King David sat on the throne until the age of 70.

So what does it mean for the righteous to "thrive like a palm tree and grow like a cedar tree in Lebanon"? Both trees are evergreens that grow slowly and consistently. The palm tree grows very straight, produces an enormous amount of fruit, and can grow as tall as 90 feet, largely because of the deep root system. Mentioned more than 70 times in the Bible, the cedars of Lebanon once shaded the entire region with heights reaching 100 feet. These trees were transported more than 200 miles from Lebanon to Jerusalem for construction of the Temple (1 Kings 6:18). As worshippers may we strive for a righteousness in our lives that allows us to take the traits of the great trees of Scripture. How do we do this? By constantly growing our relationship with Him by spending time studying Scripture, praying, telling others about Him through our stories, and doing our best to live in ways that honor Him.

prayer

Father, thank You for giving me another day to worship You. May Your spirit permeate my life and shape my heart so that my life is defined by righteousness. Allow me to grow deeper and stronger by planting the roots of my life in Your Word. Amen.

What Next?

List ways that your life can emulate the traits of the palm and cedar.

Do you consider your walk with the Lord to be "healthy and green"? Why or why not?

Day 57

Power of the Sea

*Greater than the roar of many waters—the mighty break-
ers of the sea—the LORD on high is majestic. LORD, Your
testimonies are completely reliable; holiness is the beauty
of Your house for all the days to come.*

—Psalm 93:4-5

Members of our worship choir travel regularly—for mission work, for family located across the globe, and for the
pure pleasure of going someplace new. Most have small
groups that travel together. Occasionally they join up with larger
tour groups.

One of these groups decided to take a repositioning cruise from
Dover, England, to Boston, Massachusetts. They knew there were
risks in this because of the season of the year—hurricane season.
But the ports included a favored stop in France for the Normandy
Beaches and another in Ireland. All was well for two days as they
toured Plymouth in the south of England and Normandy on the
coast of France. And then came the captain's announcement: *We
are bypassing Ireland to get ahead of an Atlantic hurricane!* The
weather picked up quickly. At times it was a really wild ride, even
though the storm was behind them. While the exterior common
places were roped off as being too dangerous, voyagers could get a
feeling for the power of the storm by watching the waves from many
of the interior public spaces. Talk about majestic—waves in a storm
like this are amazing.

It would have been easy to say the trip was a loss, but it was not.
They witnessed something unique to most cruise goers: the awesome
power of God in nature. It was a strong reminder of His majesty and
that He gathered these very seas when He laid the foundation of the
earth. Psalm 24:1-2 reminds us: "The earth and everything in it, the
world and its inhabitants, belong to the LORD; for He laid its foundation on the seas and established it on the rivers." If we agree God

did this, how can we not agree with this statement from Psalm 93? *Your testimonies are completely reliable.*

prayer

Thank You that my hope is secure in You. Forgive me when I doubt Your promises and commitments. Help my unbelief. Help me to trust in Your power. Amen.

What Next?

Where in nature have you had the kind of watershed moments described here? How did you sense God's presence?

Day 58

Who Cares?

When I am filled with cares, Your comfort brings me joy.
—*Psalm 94:19*

The psalmist seems angry as he writes. Tradition says this psalm could have been written as the Jews faced Babylonian exile. The writer had reason to be upset with the corrupt leadership. People even accused God of not seeing what was going on.

The psalmist appears to know better. He tells the people around him to pay attention. Verses 9–10 appear to call down the whiners, affirming to them that God indeed knows what's going on: "Can the One who shaped the ear not hear, the One who formed the eye not see? The One who instructs nations, the One who teaches man knowledge—does He not discipline?"

Truth hurts.

In 1960s Mississippi and other parts of the nation, the civil rights struggle reached a boiling point. It obviously did not begin then. Hate often cloaked itself part of the week in the white robes of the Klu Klux Klan who appeared as upstanding citizens in the pews of conservative churches on Sundays. If you were lucky, your parents talked to you about this as right and wrong from a biblical perspective. If you weren't taught this or did not see through the haze painted by various social strata on your own, you likely remain part of that problem today. Looking back, I realize now more than then, the unrest my parents and our friends, black and white, experienced.

I am not naïve. I know unrest continues today—some related to the subculture of the post-Civil War years and some by the add-ons of a global society. We can travel to most parts of the world in a day and can communicate to people around the globe in a matter of seconds thanks to technology. Yet, we sometimes wonder if God cares about what is going on around us. Still, this premise stands firm:

"When I am filled with cares, Your comfort brings me joy." Again, in verse 22, we are affirmed: "But the LORD is my refuge; my God is the rock of my protection."

I love Mississippi. I love how far she's come. I see how much is yet to be done. But honest people should see that about wherever they are. And if we keep God as our focus and put our personal will out of commission, we will not only be comforted in our cares, we will bring comfort and help to others.

prayer

Lord, thank You for loving me even in my disobedience. I ask forgiveness for stirring up trouble and dissension instead of spreading Your hope and Your joy and Your peace. Lord, I trust You to lead me through all of my waywardness and disobedience. Amen.

What Next?

Look deeply and honestly within yourself and at your personal and political convictions. Do they align with what you profess to believe about Jesus? If not, how can you reconcile that?

How do you share your joy when others around you are filled with sadness and concerns?

Day 59

Lord of the Sea

For the LORD is a great God, a great King above all gods.
The depths of the earth are in His hand, and the moun-
tain peaks are His. The sea is His; He made it. His hands
formed the dry land.

—Psalm 95:3–5

I remember being at the beach one summer when my children were very little. There's a picture at my house of our youngest child standing right at the water's edge with the vast ocean in front of her. I remember watching her reach down and grasp the wet sand in her chubby little hands, squishing it between her fingers, feeling the delight of it all. Seeing the juxtaposition in this picture of the tiny child and the vast, teeming ocean reminds me of what the psalmist says: "The sea is His; He made it. His hands formed the dry land."

When I consider the fact that the Rock of our salvation, the great God, the great King above all gods, the Lord our Maker—all names used by the psalmist in Psalm 95—created that vast ocean, brimming with life, I am moved to worship. Just as the psalmist seems to be. He repeatedly calls the people to action, to movement, to response: "Come, let us shout joyfully to the LORD" (v. 1); "Let us shout triumphantly" (v. 2); "Come, let us worship and bow down" (v. 6). He leads us to consider worship in our own lives. Am I allowing the greatness of our God to move me to worship? Am I mindful enough to notice the natural world around me and the image bearers I work with, play with, and live with and incline my heart to worship the Creator of it all?

The end of Psalm 95 contains an exhortation and warning. The psalmist encourages the readers to be mindful not to harden their hearts as the Israelites did at Meribah and Massah (v. 8). The stubborn Israelites (surely not like you or me, right?) grumbled, complained, tested, and simply did not trust the Lord—the God who delivered them from slavery and provided for their every need.

If we're honest, we see those tendencies in our own lives. I know I see them in mine. Let's pray that our hearts will instead be inclined toward worship.

prayer

Thank You, Lord, that You are the Rock of our salvation. That there is no element of our world that You did not form with Your own hands. Thank You that we are Your people, the flock under Your care. Help us to trust You, because You are worthy of our trust and our worship. Amen.

What Next?

What in the natural world most moves you to worship?

In what ways do you test, complain, or grumble against God? How can cultivating a response of worship to His creation help fight these tendencies?

Day 60

It All Begins with Worship

Let the heavens be glad and the earth rejoice; let the sea and all that fills it resound. Let the fields and everything in them exult. Then all the trees of the forest will shout for joy.

—Psalm 96:11–12

O ur choir loves composer Benjamin Harlan. Not only are his arrangements great, he makes the choir laugh. One of their favorite things for him to do is to sit at the piano and teach a difficult song. It really doesn't matter how hard the notes, lyrics, or rhythm are—with Benjie, it becomes music and fun! Some choral directors have been known to give up teaching an arrangement because of its difficulty. Not Benjie.

Several years ago I watched him do this with a choral arrangement based on Isaiah 55:12: "You will indeed go out with joy and be peacefully guided; the mountains and the hills will break into singing before you, and all the trees of the field will clap their hands." Although it was enormously difficult, it was worth it! In the end it became a choir favorite and forever etched that verse in our hearts and minds.

The main theme of that verse is also found in Psalm 96. This is likely another of David's psalms. It also looks forward rather than giving a backward look based on his experiences. And it is all about worship! In fact, the first three verses of Psalm 96 are definitely a call to worship: Sing . . . Sing . . . Sing! Tell all the nations about the glorious nature of God, tell them of His good works and that He is the source of our salvation.

As David wrote Psalm 96, under Jewish law the Gentiles were not allowed to worship in the heart of the Temple. In Psalm 96, the psalmist points toward that day when Jesus made it clear He came for all of us when He gave us the Great Commission in Matthew 28:18–20: "Then Jesus came near and said to them, 'All authority has been given to Me in heaven and on earth. Go, therefore, and make disciples of all nations, baptizing them in the name of the Father and of the Son and of the Holy Spirit, teaching them to observe everything I have commanded you. And remember, I am with you always, to the end of the age.'"

Psalm 96:4-6 tells us why He will be with us to the end of the age.

> *For the LORD is great and is highly praised; He is feared above all gods. For all the gods of the peoples are idols, but the LORD made the heavens. Splendor and majesty are before Him; strength and beauty are in His sanctuary.*

Any other god is nothing but an idol. Our God is the One True God who made everything—so praise Him and worship Him. David then tells us in verses 7-9 that in our worship we must "ascribe"—give Him credit—for our families, for any glory and strength, and *the glory of His name.* Finally, we are told to worship—all of creation will worship Him!

prayer

Lord, I thank You for teaching me how to worship. Thank You for commanding me to worship because You know I need it to be in line with what You want for me. Forgive me when I ignore Your desire to spend time with me. Amen.

What Next?

Meditate verse by verse on Psalm 96. Record what each verse teaches you about worship.

Day 61

Are You Worshipping Worship?

*All who serve carved images, those who boast in idols, will
be put to shame. All the gods must worship Him.*

—Psalm 97:7

Imagine for a moment you arrive at church this Sunday. You have
your Bible in hand and family in tow and are ready for a great
day of worship. As you enter the worship center, things look like
any other Sunday: preservice music is playing, people are greeting
one another, the worship band is ready to go. At the appointed hour,
however, things get weird. The worship leader steps into position
carrying a statue, a golden calf just like the one you learned about
as a child in Sunday School, and places it in the center of the platform. As the congregation audibly gasps, the worship leader invites
the congregation to stand and worship this thing, this inanimate
object that carries no power or hope. Two things then happen: First,
several deacons rush the platform, remove the idol, and chase the
worship leader out the front door. Second, a medical team rushes
to the pastor with a defibrillator unit to resuscitate him following
cardiac arrest!

While this situation may seem ludicrous, it is closer to reality
than we might want to believe. In truth, we live in a land of idol
worshippers. Over the past 30 years, a monumental shift of focus
has placed a growing emphasis on the topic of worship, giving rise to
countless books and articles, a plethora of conferences and training
events, a new genre of worship consultants, as well as parachurch
organizations and entire publishing houses singularly dedicated to
the subject. Colleges and seminaries now offer degrees in worship
studies/leadership. The subject of worship, almost without fail, sur-
faces in any church-related discussion.

At first glance this is not bad. After all, God instructed us to
worship Him. It is theologically problematic when our *approach to
worship* displaces the *object of worship*. Unfortunately, it is easy

to find ourselves focusing on the wrong thing. While we have not forged literal idols, far too many of us have elevated our methodology of worship to golden calf status, sanctimoniously placing it on the altars of our churches. Our intentions may be honorable, but an idol is still an idol, and the end result is exactly the same!

When did we become idol worshippers? It happened when the method of worship became the priority of our churches. Many spend much more time promoting a style of worship over encouraging people to stand in the presence of God—in whatever form that may take. And a lot of us have bought into the idea. This coming weekend countless people will leave our worship services and comment, "I loved the worship today," when they really mean they loved the music. Therein lies the problem: our churches are filled with people hungry for a specific worship style (traditional, contemporary, modern, alternative, coffeehouse, or whatever else) rather than a life-changing dialogue with God. In elevating musical styles, our churches have polarized the bride of Christ, and there is no one to blame but ourselves.

In Exodus 20:3 when God said, "Do not have other gods besides Me," He meant it! This means literally nothing should take importance over the One True God. God so desires to have communion with us that He never allows anything to be placed above Him.

prayer

Father, forgive me for placing my preferences above You. I ask that You place a desire in my soul to encounter You fresh today. Shine Your face upon me. In Jesus' name. Amen.

What Next?

Honestly evaluate the role music style plays in your worship. Has style become an idol in your life?

$\mathcal{D}ay$ 62

The Lord Is Come

Shout to the LORD, all the earth; be jubilant, shout for joy, and sing. . . . Let the rivers clap their hands; let the mountains shout together for joy before the LORD, for he is coming to judge the earth.

—Psalm 98:4–9

I f you have ever sung from a hymn book in your church, you've probably sung a song by Isaac Watts. Watts wrote more than 600 hymns and become known as the Father of English Hymnody.

In his early hymns, Watts paraphrased the psalms by "Christianizing" their Jewish context. Because Jesus fulfilled the messianic prophecies of the Old Testament, Watts changed the future tense verbs in the psalms to present tense. The world was no longer anticipating the Messiah . . . He has come in the person of Jesus Christ!

Though not originally intended as a Christmas hymn, "Joy to the World" became one of the most beloved carols in the world. Based on Psalm 98, it is an excellent example of how Watts paraphrased the psalms through the lens of the Cross and Christ's victory over sin, death, and the grave.

Psalm 98:9: "For He is coming to judge the earth. He will judge the world righteously and the peoples fairly."

Hymn: "Joy to the world the Lord is come"

Psalm 98:5-6: "Sing unto the LORD with the lyre; with the lyre and melodious song. With trumpets and the blast of the ram's horn shout triumphantly in the presence of the LORD, our King."

Hymn: "Joy to the earth, the Savior reigns! Let men their songs employ"

Psalm 98:7-8: "Let the sea and all that fills it, the world and those that live in it, resound. Let the rivers clap their hands; let the mountains shout together for joy."

Hymn: "While fields and floods, rocks, hills and plains, repeat the sounding joy"

prayer

Father in heaven, thank You allowing Your Son, Jesus Christ, to bring joy to this world! Today we join with the hills and seas in singing our song of praise to You. May Your Word take on new meaning in my life, and may the way I live my life today vividly reflect the joy I have in You. Amen.

What Next?

Take time today to paraphrase Psalm 98 based on your life and experiences. It will change the way you view this Psalm for the rest of your life.

Day 63

Still Choosing Joy

Shout triumphantly to the LORD, all the earth. Serve the LORD with gladness; come before Him with joyful songs. Acknowledge that Yahweh is God. He made us, and we are His—His people, the sheep of His pasture. Enter His gates with thanksgiving and His courts with praise. Give thanks to Him and praise His name. For Yahweh is good, and His love is eternal; His faithfulness endures through all generations.

—Psalm 100:1-5

C hoices are decisions you make. A consequence of your choices may be the circumstances you find yourself in after the decision is made. Your circumstances may also be a product of heredity or someone else's bad choice. Nonetheless, you may find yourself in a bad place at times. How you respond to it speaks volumes to those around you about your relationship to God and, in truth, the authenticity of your worship.

A friend once told me that survival of the nastiness of life requires you to continuously choose joy. Her approach is to address life's challenges head on, rely on her relationship with God, and rest in His love. She believes that going through the motions with God is not enough and that you must make deliberate choices as you cling to Him. She also knows from experience that people observe how you respond in the hard times of life. You must choose to be joyful even when it is difficult to do so. You must express your joy to the Lord and be thankful in the circumstances where you are. Sure, you can pray for a change in those circumstances, but to be joyful in those circumstances and to shout that joy triumphantly to the Lord requires effort. Joy does not just happen—it is a choice.

In Galatians 5:22-23, Paul tells us joy is an attribute of a Christian. We must choose joy to live for Christ and worship Him fully:

But the fruit of the Spirit is love, joy, peace, patience, kindness, goodness, faith, gentleness, self-control. Against such things there is no law.

In John 15:9–11, we discover that for God's love to manifest in us and complete us, we must remain in His love—yet another choice we must make as it will not be made for us:

As the Father has loved Me, I have also loved you. Remain in My love. If you keep My commands you will remain in My love, just as I have kept My Father's commands and remain in His love. I have spoken these things to you so that My joy may be in you and your joy may be complete.

You don't choose joy once and thereafter assume you've been there and done that. You must still choose joy every day in every circumstance. Psalm 100 even describes how choosing joy becomes a product of our living completely for Jesus—shout to Him in worship (even if you cannot sing most everyone can shout!); serve Him; come to Him first always, acknowledge His presence, find where He is at work and enter in; thank Him; and praise His name.

prayer

Lord, thank You for teaching me to choose joy through all circumstances. Use me to show others what a difference this makes in my relationship with You and with them. Amen

What Next?

Meditate on the seven actions of Psalm 100—shout, serve, come, acknowledge, enter, thank, and praise.

Record in your journal the circumstances of your life where you struggle with any of these and steps you can take to make choosing joy a continuous part of your worship.

Day 64

Choosing Wisely

No one who acts deceitfully will live in my palace; no one who tells lies will remain in my presence.

—Psalm 101:7

Author Ethel Watts Mumford said, "God gave us our relatives; thank God we can choose our friends." Too often we underestimate the influence of those around us on our decisions, actions, and words. My girls have heard it all their lives. In fact, they now simply quote it to me. Each time they left the house I would admonish them with a challenge: remember who you are and *whose* you are. The implications are obvious. My daughters carried my name. More importantly, as children of the Most High God, they belonged to Him through the blood of Jesus. To bring dishonor to either was unacceptable.

In Psalm 101, the newly ascended King David basically lays down the law as to who he will allow to influence him. Straightforward and to the point, this psalm is a type of friend filter that helps us draw boundaries in our lives. David committed to the following:

I will not look at worthless things.

I will not be around those who slander their neighbor.

I will not be involved with evil.

I will not tolerate haughty eyes or arrogance.

I will not have deceivers near me.

I will not have liars in my presence.

I will sing of His faithful love.

I will sing of His justice.

I will sing praise.

I will live with a heart of integrity.

I will hate the practice of transgression.

I will keep a devious heart far from me.

I will keep my eyes on the faithful.

I will destroy the wicked.

I will eliminate evildoers from my presence.

As worshippers, this list is especially important. David includes actions that break our relationship with God and steal our song. There also are behaviors that protect our hearts and keep us focused on God. This battle is ongoing and must be fought each day. As Paul reminds us in Galatians 5:17, "For the flesh desires what is against the Spirit, and the Spirit desires what is against the flesh; these are opposed to each other, so that you don't do what you want."

Draw the boundaries in your life. Our worship is much too important!

prayer

Father, allow my life to be blameless in Your sight. Give me the strength to embrace the attributes in Psalm 101 and the courage to eliminate things breaking my relationship with You. Amen.

What Next?

Read 1 Thessalonians 4:1–12. Now reread Psalm 101. What are the similarities?

Take a few minutes to identify your three closest friends. Now run them through the filter of this psalm.

Day 65

The Great Equalizer

*As for man, his days are like grass—he blooms like a
flower of the field; when the wind passes over it, it van-
ishes, and its place is no longer known.*

—Psalm 103:15

*Every man must do two things alone; he must do his own
believing and his own dying. —Martin Luther*

*It is not death that a man should fear, but he should fear
never beginning to live. —Marcus Aurelius*

*I would rather die a meaningful death than to live a
meaningless life. —Corazon Aquino*

*A friend of mine stopped smoking, drinking, overeating,
and chasing women—all at the same time. It was a lovely
funeral. —Unknown*

*Most people can't bear to sit in church for an hour on
Sundays. How are they supposed to live somewhere very
similar to it for eternity? —Mark Twain*

*It's not that I'm afraid to die, I just don't want to be there
when it happens. —Woody Allen*

People approach death with all different types of attitudes—
fear, complacency, even humor humor. A number of years
ago, I attended a funeral where the deceased had the
distinction of having her ex-husbands as pall bearers . . . all five of
them! A family of avid hunters, everyone in the funeral processional
wore camouflage hunting attire. But it didn't stop there. As the
family filed past the body to pay their final respects, I noticed they
were placing small objects inside the casket. As I got closer I realized the casket was full of turkey calls, little gadgets hunters use
to imitate the sound of turkeys. You can't make this stuff up!

Death is no respecter of persons. It doesn't discriminate based on age, social status, or gender. It's the great equalizer. Psalm 103:15 reminds us of the brevity of life. Like a flower bloom tossed in the wind, so is life. But for the Christian, death brings no fear. When Jesus came forth from the tomb, He defeated death and the grave. This is why the Apostle Paul declares:

> *Death has been swallowed up in victory. Death, where is your victory? Death, where is your sting? Now the sting of death is sin, and the power of sin is the law. But thanks be to God, who gives us the victory through our Lord Jesus Christ!*
>
> —*1 Corinthians 15:54–57*

Billy Graham once said, "The way we view death determines, to a surprising degree, the way we live our lives." This being true, may we as believers live our lives in the confidence of the truth that death was no match for our Lord. Through Him death has died!

prayer

Eternal Father, teach us to number our days so that we may live wisely. Allow us to view death not as an end but as the moment we fully know You. We thank You for the victory over death and for assuring us that death does not have the last word. Amen.

What Next?

Take a few minutes to write about the legacy you would leave if you died today. How do you think you would be remembered?

Day 66

Faithful in Adversity

He had sent a man ahead of them—Joseph, who was sold as a slave.

—Psalm 105:17

On the evening of April 14, 1865, John Parker was assigned the seemingly inconsequential task of guarding the entrance to a private box at the local theater. Although a veteran officer with the Metropolitan Police Department of the District of Columbia, Parker left his post that night and visited a nearby tavern. With the door left unguarded, John Wilkes Booth entered the Presidential Box at Ford's Theatre and fired a single shot into the head of President Abraham Lincoln, immediately altering the course of American history.

As the winds from Hurricane Isabel swept across Arlington National Cemetery on September 18, 2003, Sergeant First Class Fredrick Geary and other members of the Old Guard assigned to stand watch over the Tomb of the Unknowns faced a dilemma. Would they remain at their assigned post in the onslaught of the storm or seek shelter until the danger subsided? During that storm-filled night, surrounded by lightning strikes and falling trees, Geary and his fellow guards never faltered. Drenched and pummeled by the ceaseless rain and wind, the guards marched their well-known 21 steps, putting duty and honor before their own safety. One reporter wrote, "It reminded all that their lone walk before a marble sarcophagus was not merely a job, but a *calling* and honor not to be easily cast aside or abandoned for momentary convenience."

These two events remind us that being faithful to our calling and showing up—no matter what—makes a difference! Far too many Christians are willing to stay away from corporate worship for virtually any reason, demonstrating commitment levels that more closely resemble John Parker than the vigilant soldiers of the Old

Guard. Too often we are simply derelict of duty, abandoning our posts with little thought.

Joseph is a great example of faithfulness through adversity. After his brothers betrayed him and sold him into slavery, Joseph could have given up . . . but he didn't. Instead, he remained committed to God, eventually rising to the highest levels of authority in Egypt. From this position, God used Joseph to accomplish His will in the lives of the children of Israel and to fulfill his covenant to Abraham (Genesis 17).

Satan is an old pro at convincing folks they aren't needed. He fills our thoughts with the likes of, "I'm too busy," or, "No one will miss me." The deceiver does this for a reason: when worship is weakened, the church is rendered ineffective.

prayer

Eternal Father, renew in my heart a desire to worship with God's people. I understand the church is empowered through worship and attacks the adversary through authentic worship. I commit to be faithful with my presence and to stand guard as we share the gospel with a world in need of Jesus. Amen.

What Next?

The God of the universe placed a powerful calling on each of us as worshippers to lead His church into battle each week. Today, embrace that calling and commit to be in your place as part of the body of Christ.

Simply showing up can make the difference, in this world and the next, in someone's life.

$\mathcal{D}ay$ 67

Great Movements of God

At Horeb they made a calf and worshiped the cast metal image. They exchanged their glory for the image of a grass-eating ox.

—Psalm 106:19–20

W hat do the following events have in common?

The Day of Pentecost (30 AD)

The Reformation (1517–1648)

The First Great Awakening (1727–1755)

The Jesus Movement (1967–1975)

Each was an incredible movement of God. Acts 2 records that on the Day of Pentecost more than 3,000 people were saved, and the world was never the same! In 1517, Martin Luther penned his Ninety-Five Theses, birthing Protestantism and forever changing the face of Christianity. During the First Great Awakening, thousands flocked to hear the preaching of Jonathan Edwards and George Whitefield. It is estimated more than 50,000 people came to faith in Jesus in New England alone. Beginning in the late 1960s, the Jesus movement reached an estimated 300,000 with the gospel and changed the way churches approached an entire generation.

Great movements of God share a common thread: they are always preceded by worship.

Moses led the people of Israel out of Egypt *after* he met God in the burning bush.

Jonah went to Nineveh *after* he met God in the belly of a fish.

Goliath fell *after* David worshipped God in the fields outside Bethlehem.

The Holy Spirit descended on the Day of Pentecost *after* Jesus restored Peter on the shores of the Sea of Galilee.

Christianity spread across the globe *after* Paul met the risen Lord on the road to Damascus.

Psalm 106:19–23 references another event when worship preceded a supernatural movement of God. When Moses was delayed in coming down from Mount Horeb, the Israelites pressured Aaron into making a golden calf for them to worship. An angry God informed Moses He would destroy the Israelites, but Moses stood in the gap for them. Moses, however, understood that without God's presence, the people could not survive, and he *begged* God to stay with them. He then made a bold request of God in Exodus 33:18: "Please, let me see your glory."

What would happen if God showed us His glory? How would it impact your family? Your church? Your personal walk with the Lord? God desires to show us His glory . . . but not on our terms. We will only experience His presence when we fall on our faces before God, repent of our sinfulness, and then, like Moses, beg God to show us His glory. When He does, our lives will never be the same!

prayer

Holy God, show us Your glory. As Your holy presence fills our lives may it illuminate every corner and crevice of our being. When Your glory passes by may our lives be forever altered for Your honor. Amen.

What Next?

Remember that great movements of God begin with worship. The question is not whether God can show His glory but rather are we willing to do what's necessary for it to happen? What needs to change in your life for you to be worthy of seeing God's glory?

Day 68
Are You in a Desert?

Some wandered in the desolate wilderness, finding no way to a city where they could live. They were hungry and thirsty; their spirits failed within them. Then they cried out to the LORD in their trouble; He rescued them from their distress.

—Psalm 107:4-6

I've always been fascinated by the Exodus. If you've ever watched *The Ten Commandments*, the scene where Moses (Charlton Heston) leads the children of Israel across the Red Sea is probably seared in your mind. Amazingly, almost immediately after being delivered from the Egyptians, the people start to complain . . . about *everything!*

They complained even though God was with them in a pillar of cloud by day and a pillar of fire by night (Exodus 13:17-22).

They complained about the water (Exodus 15:22-26).

They complained about having no food, accusing Moses of bringing them into the wilderness to die of hunger.

They complained when there was no water, saying God had brought them and their livestock into the wilderness to die of thirst.

The Israelites didn't wander in the wilderness for 40 years because they were lost. The geographical area is relatively small and could have been navigated quickly, even back then. They were probably simply going in circles. I'm sure at some point someone said, "I think we've seen that camel before!" *They certainly were not lost.*

So why did they wander? Scripture is clear: the people wandered in the wilderness because of their *murmuring and complaining.* Although God never left them, He used the wilderness experience as a time of teaching, spiritual growth, and punishment.

Remember, God despises mouths that complain. Unfortunately, it's far too easy to adopt a critical spirit that spews forth negativity and pessimism impacting everything—and everyone—around us! Developing and maintaining a closeness with God, as well as those who mentor us and hold us accountable, can all help us avoid developing such a critical nature. And remember: wilderness worship is labored and routine.

prayer

Jesus, thank You for Your Word today. Forgive me for my tendency to murmur and complain. Give me courage today to stand against negativity, focus my mind on the hope of Your presence, and allow me to have a positive impact on those around me. Amen.

What Next?

Are you in the wilderness? What about your church? Are you bitter and ungrateful? What is your golden calf? Has your focus moved there and away from Him? If so, your thoughts and words become critical, your heart darkened, your worship weak, and your life characterized by powerlessness and a lack of God's supernatural presence.

Take time to confess the sin of negativity, and ask God to fill your mind with the hope that comes through His presence.

Day 69

A King and a Priest

This is the declaration of the LORD to my Lord: "Sit at
My right hand until I make Your enemies Your footstool."
—Psalm 110:1

David is an enigma. The circumstances bringing him from humble boy shepherd to giant slayer to the first anointed king of Israel would probably make one big-time epic movie. David, in writing Psalm 110, emphasized both the kingship of Jesus and the eternal priesthood. Somehow, in his spirit, David understood all that.

In fact, I was thinking recently how the Easter spiritual "Were You There?" would be perfect thematic music for David's story as he prophetically describes his relationship to Christ the King. Talk about epic! Most folks know the words to this hymn:

Were you there when they crucified my Lord?
Were you there when they nailed him to the tree?
Were you there when they laid him in the tomb?
Were you there when God rose him from the tomb?

The underscore of this arrangement takes you through the dark hours to the ultimate promise—*He arose!*—just as He said He would, conquering death to reign forever, as Psalm 110 suggests.

Psalm 110 is the most well known of the ten royal psalms. These psalms all point to God's promise to David that his kingdom had an eternal connection. They point to the Messiah. In 1 Chronicles 17, David received God's Covenant concerning his descendants, culminating in God's promise of an eternal connection through David's house:

I will be a father to him, and he will be a son to Me. I will not take away My faithful love from him as I took it from the one who was before you. I will appoint him over My house and My kingdom forever, and his throne will be established forever.

—vv.13-14

As Jesus approached the awful events preceding His death, He faced the Pharisees with a question for the ages. Matthew 22:41-46 tells that story, using David's words from Psalm 110:1:

While the Pharisees were together, Jesus questioned them, "What do you think about the Messiah? Whose Son is He?" "David's," they told Him. He asked them, "How is it then that David, inspired by the Spirit, calls Him 'Lord': The Lord declared to my Lord, 'Sit at My right hand until I put Your enemies under Your feet'? If David calls Him 'Lord,' how then can the Messiah be his Son?" No one was able to answer Him at all, and from that day no one dared to question Him anymore.

God's covenant with David was confirmed when Jesus came and died and rose again. The Lord of the universe sent His Son, our Lord, to earth to save us. As David did, we should worship Him today.

prayer

Lord, forgive me when I want my way and want to proclaim my destiny. Help me to understand Your promises and accept and share with others the truth of them. Amen.

What Next?

Search the Gospels for other references to Psalm 110:1. In context, how were these words used to affirm God's Covenant with David?

Day 70

Extravagant Worship

Hallelujah! I will praise the LORD with all my heart in the assembly of the upright and in the congregation.
—Psalm 111:1

Have you heard of someone willing to sacrifice everything for someone else? World War II, while one of the darkest periods in American history, forged many heroes like this. First Lieutenant John R. Fox was such a man. In December 1944, Fox volunteered to stay behind in a small Italian village when American troops were forced to withdraw after being overrun by a surprise German attack. From his position on the second floor of a local house, Fox called for defensive artillery fire to hold off the Germans. Unfortunately, this did not deter the German soldiers, and their attack intensified. As the Germans advanced closer to the center of the village, Fox radioed instructions for the artillery strikes to shift closer and closer to his position. This tactic delayed the German offensive and gave Fox's troops the chance to retreat and reform their unit. Although the members of his infantry unit were now safe, the Germans continued to close in on Fox's position. He, to the stunned surprise of the soldier receiving the message, radioed to again have the fire moved even closer. When he was informed this was basically suicide since the artillery shells would land directly on his position, Fox simply replied, "Fire it." When his men eventually retook the position, they found Fox's body next to nearly 100 dead German troops.

In Psalm 111:1, the writer commits to worship with this same level of exuberance: "I will praise the LORD with *all* my heart" (author's emphasis). He comes before the Lord with everything. His attitude is defined by an all-consuming extravagance.

In John 12 we see another example of extravagant worship. Less than a week before Jesus would die, He came to Bethany to visit his old friend, Lazarus. As they reclined at the table eating dinner,

Mary, Lazarus's sister, took a pound of expensive perfume, anointed Jesus' feet, and then wiped His feet with her hair. Mary knew exactly who Jesus was. She had sat at His feet and heard His teaching and probably helped remove the burial clothes from Lazarus's body after Jesus raised him from the dead. But not everyone was happy. As the fragrance of the oil filled the house, Judas, and probably others, began to complain about waste . . . the extravagance.

The disciples didn't understand, but Mary did. Within a week Jesus would be dead, His body once again anointed with spices and oil and laid in a borrowed tomb. Mary's love for Jesus was demonstrated with an act of extravagant worship without regard of the opinion of others. Is your worship characterized by total abandon or thoughtless ritual? He deserves our everything . . . will you give it?

prayer

Lord, forgive me for the many times I have only gone through the motions of worship. Allow me to respond to You with my total being . . . everything I have . . . in an extravagant offering of praise. In the name of Jesus. Amen.

What's Next?

Describe what worshipping with all your heart would look like. What would it cost you to make that happen? What sacrifices would you have to make?

Day 71

The Glory of Creation

From the rising of the sun to its setting, let the name of Yahweh be praised.

—Psalm 113:3

Not much stresses me out, but the process of buying a house is an exception. Several years ago, after months of searching the Internet, hours of driving by potential properties, and countless walk-throughs, we (or should I say my wife Wendy) finally made an offer. What prompted her to choose *this* house? The sunsets. Because the house is situated on a lake, dusk ushers in a completely unique experience accented with a vast array of colors and geometric designs, all displayed in high definition across a vast celestial canvas. Each sunset is an artistic masterpiece, and they're all in full view from our den. No wonder Wendy chose this house! After several days of experiencing this nightly art exhibit I came to a sobering conclusion: I've missed far too many sunsets during my life.

Psalm 113:4–6 references in poetic detail our response of praise to Yahweh, the Creator of the Universe:

Yahweh is exalted above all the nations, His glory above the heavens. Who is like Yahweh our God—the One enthroned on high, who stoops down to look on the heavens and the earth?

Think about it. Everything . . . created from nothing. The Creator spoke everything into existence: the sun and moon, stars, oceans, towering trees, plants, fish, animals, insects, and sunsets. As worshippers, we simply have to look around us to see God's magnificent glory displayed in breathtaking majesty. Even more amazingly, all of it is visible in a sunset. We simply must slow down enough to see it.

prayer

Father Creator, I wait today with eager anticipation for what You have in store for me. I confess that too many times, my life is out of control. Slow down my mind and body enough so I don't miss what You have for me today. Thank You for waking me this morning with another opportunity to worship You through Your creation. Allow me to take full advantage of this gift . . . *especially* tonight's sunset. Amen.

What Next?

Today will probably be busy. In fact, it might even be stressful. Make a commitment right now to set aside 30 minutes tonight to have a cup of coffee, find an unobstructed view, and experience the beauty of creation as the Master Artist presents one incredible display of His majesty and power. It's amazing what you can learn from a sunset!

Day 72

Becoming What We Worship

*Their idols are silver and gold, made by human hands.
. . . Those who make them are just like them, as are all who
trust in them.*

—*Psalm 115:4–8*

P eople do strange things. *The Chicago Tribune* once reported
of a New Mexico woman who, while frying tortillas, noticed
the skillet burn marks left on the tortilla formed what
she thought appeared to be the image of Christ. She immediately
removed the tortilla, and after consulting family and friends, carried it to her priest who reluctantly agreed the image resembled
that of Jesus. The perplexed priest blessed the tortilla, after which
the lady carried it home. She placed the tortilla in a plastic frame
and set it on a mass of cotton, giving the image of Jesus floating
on cloud. Curious visitors soon began flocking to her home. By the
time the *Chicago Tribune* article published, more than 8,000 people
had passed through the house to view the image of Christ in the
tortilla. Most observers agreed the image bore some resemblance to
what they imagined Christ looked like, though one reporter said it
looked a lot like former heavyweight boxing champion Leon Spinks!

This story reminds us that everyone worships something . . . and
some people will worship anything. This should come as no surprise
to Christians. We were created with a void in our lives, an empty
place that only can be filled by God. People try to fill this void with
all sorts of things (fame, relationships, money), but none of these
works. The empty place remains simply because it can only be filled
by God. Only through real worship, an aggressive love relationship
with God that glorifies Him, can the void in our lives be filled.

I have a T-shirt bearing the caption: "Jesus Is Not Religion." Most
of us try to substitute things, many of them good, in the place only
He can fill. This never works. What God desires most is that we
pursue Him . . . *passionately!* In Matthew 22, the Pharisees faced

the same dilemma when they asked Jesus, "What command in the law is the greates?" (v. 36). (They were most concerned about what was *the* most important thing in their lives—most likely not in a spiritual sense!) Jesus responded, "Love the Lord your God with all your heart, with all your soul, and will all your mind" (v. 37). Jesus reminds us nothing (rules, church attendance, morals, wealth, service and good works, anything) is more important than knowing and loving Him.

A quotation attributed to Ralph Waldo Emerson underscores this idea, "A person will worship something, have no doubt about it. We may think our tribute is paid in secret in the dark recesses of our hearts, but it will come out. That which dominates our imaginations and our thoughts will determine our lives and our character. Therefore, it behooves us to be careful what we worship . . . for what we are worshipping we are becoming."

What are you worshipping? You need to know because that's what you are becoming.

prayer

Father, protect me from attempting to fill my life with things other than You. May I live every moment with a sense of urgency to remain close to Your heart, held by the unwavering grip of Your love. I pray my life will bring honor to Your name and spread Your fame. Amen.

What Next?

What are you becoming? Have you substituted religion for a relationship? Is the desire of your heart to know Him more intimately? Do you passionately pursue His character? Only when we know Him in His fullness do we experience true transformation . . . and only then can we become what God intended us to be.

Day 73

Praise Him!

Praise the LORD, all nations! Glorify Him, all peoples! For His faithful love to us is great; the LORD's faithfulness endures forever. Hallelujah!

—Psalm 117:1-2

When I read Psalm 117 (in my mind it is always in the King James Version that I memorized as a child), I hear the chorus of "To God Be the Glory," the great hymn of Fanny Crosby:

Praise the Lord, praise the Lord, let the earth hear His voice;
Praise the Lord, praise the Lord, let the people rejoice;
O come to the Father through Jesus the Son,
And give Him the glory; great things He hath done.

Sometimes good things really do come in small packages. Psalm 117 is the shortest of all the psalms. It is also the 595th of the 1,189 chapters of the King James Bible, making it the middle chapter and the shortest chapter in that version of the Bible. Psalm 117 is one of the psalms of the *Hallel* (Psalms 113–118), which are recited as one in a song of praise by the Jews on their joyous holy days.

Notice, though, this psalm does not limit praise and worship to the Jews. All nations—everybody—are invited to join in and worship the God of all! We don't know who penned the words to this great psalm, but it was someone who inherently understood that God was the God of all the nations.

Paul and Peter in the New Testament made it clear that God did intend for the gospel to be for all people. We are not that different. So many Christians today somehow decided we are not responsible for telling others about Jesus. Instead, we just want to be fed, or in some cases, only be culturally acknowledged as Christians. That is so wrong!

Almost begrudgingly, Peter says to the Gentiles in Acts 10:28, "You know it's forbidden for a Jewish man to associate with or visit a foreigner. But God has shown me that I must not call any person common or unclean."

Paul reminds us in Galatians 3:16 of a promise God made to Abraham in Genesis: "Now the promises were spoken to Abraham and to his seed. He does not say 'and to seeds,' as though referring to many, but referring to one, and to your seed, who is Christ.'"

Paul goes on in verses 28–29: "There is no Jew or Greek, slave or free, male or female; for you are all one in Christ Jesus. And if you belong to Christ, then you are Abraham's seed, heirs according to the promise."

So, since we all belong to Christ—Jew or Gentile, regardless of nation or station in life or circumstance—let us all praise the Lord together and be thankful that His love is great and endures forever.

prayer

Lord, I praise You today. Thank You for Your faithfulness. Forgive my disobedience in failing to share You with others around me. Give me boldness in my convictions. Amen.

What Next?

Tell someone about Jesus today. Record who, where, and when in your journal.

Read God's call of Abraham in Genesis 12:1–3. What was his response? How did he praise the Lord?

Day 74

Inside Out

I have treasured Your word in my heart so that I may not sin against You.

—Psalm 119:11

Your word is a lamp for my feet and a light on my path.
—Psalm 119:105

I am a fan of starting our kids young on memorizing Scripture. I am thankful for the days of Royal Ambassadors, Bible Drill, children and youth choirs, and, back in the days, in public school choir and at times in the classroom.

Those words memorized long ago are the passages I come back to time and again as I travel down life's road. They come to mind without thinking about it when I face many different things. They wake me up at night, calm me down, and even get me fired up for worship.

I heard a young minister of music tell a story about his dad. His father was dealing with significant medical issues and had been hospitalized for a while. When he arrived to be with him, the nursing staff told him amazing things his dad, who was marginally conscious, had said out loud. He quoted Scripture to them. Apparently, he quoted volumes of it. God's Word was what he carried within himself, and it is what came out even when he had very limited control of his faculties. I will never forget hearing that story and have often wondered to myself what I would do if it were me in that hospital bed. What would be coming out from within me?

Being a history buff, I was drawn to Laura Hillenbrand's book *Unbroken*, the biography of Olympian and WWII veteran Louis Zamperini, who survived a plane crash, 47 days in the Pacific, and cruel treatment in a Japanese POW camp. Returning home, alcohol and depression plagued him. On the verge of leaving him, his wife was saved at a Billy Graham crusade, and by some miracle, got him to go. He left his first time there in anger but returned another night. That night he committed his life to Jesus. He recalled promises made to God while floating in the Pacific hoping for rescue, promises long since forgotten. Zamperini returned to Japan and ministered to those who had been his captors, leading many of them to Christ. God's word now hidden in his heart showed him the way to forgiveness.

prayer

Lord, forgive me for internalizing things that don't matter or that do not glorify You. Discipline me to stay in Your Word and follow where Your Word leads me. Amen.

What Next?

What Scripture have you memorized lately? Write it down.

Commit to learn a new passage (even in a song if that helps) weekly. Track those in your journal, and revisit them often.

Day 75

Give Me Peace

In my distress I called to the LORD, and He answered me. "LORD, deliver me from lying lips and a deceitful tongue."

—Psalm 120:1-2

Some images are impossible to forget. Prior to Game 3 of the 2001 World Series, President George W. Bush ascended the mound at Yankee Stadium. Surrounded by deafening applause and chants of "USA! USA!" Bush gave a thumbs up and delivered the first pitch with a strike to the catcher. It was described by reporters as "much more than a ceremonial first pitch. It was a signal to the country that healing could begin after the 9/11 attacks." Just a few weeks earlier, the tragic events of September 11, 2001, rocked the foundation of the nation and defined New York City as a city in distress. On this night, however, healing began.

This same type of national sentiment, simultaneously marked by desperation and hope, permeates the 15 psalms known as the Songs of Ascents (120-134). Serving as a biblical GPS, these psalms allow us to walk with Israel on her 70-year journey from exile to Jerusalem. Most scholars believe the Songs of Ascent were sung by travelers making their way up to Jerusalem for the major Jewish feasts of Passover, Pentecost, and Tabernacles, pilgrimages required every year for all Jewish men according to the Law. We also know the walk of several days from Nazareth to Jerusalem was a familiar journey for Jesus and His family:

Every year His parents traveled to Jerusalem for the Passover Festival. When He was 12 years old, they went up according to the custom of the festival. After those days were over, as they were returning, the boy Jesus stayed behind in Jerusalem, but His parents did not know it.

—Luke 2:41-43

On this journey through the hillsides surrounding Jerusalem, Jewish pilgrims would unite their voices in song while straining their eyes for the first glimpses of the Holy City. The Songs of Ascents gave them a shared experience, reflecting on God's works in the past while celebrating the hope of the future. Once in Jerusalem, the weary traveler made their ascent up the 15 steps leading to the Temple, pausing to sing one song per step, beginning with Psalm 120 on the first step and ending with Psalm 134 on the top.

As the journey begins in Psalm 120, the psalmist vividly paints a picture of the deep level of distress rising from exile. He finds himself captive in a land he despises hoping for a better day that seems beyond reach. Have you ever found yourself in a situation that seems hopeless? Are you in spiritual exile? If so, how do you respond? Like the psalmist, in our distress, we can call to the Lord having full confidence He will answer. This truth makes exile a little easier to endure.

prayer

Great Comforter, thank You for allowing Your presence to be felt in time of spiritual exile in my life. I confess that sometimes my despair during life's journey seems insurmountable, but I'm thankful the hope provided by Your presence in my life. I ask that You make it especially felt in my life today. Amen.

What Next?

List three things that put your soul in spiritual exile.

How can personal and corporate worship help you navigate these times?

Day 76

I Lift My Eyes

I lift up my eyes toward the mountains. Where will my help come from? My help comes from the LORD, the Maker of heaven and earth."

—*Psalm 121:1-2*

God blessed me with a large extended family. Our gatherings were huge, often exceeding 100 when we were all together. And we self-entertained since everyone loved to sing and play instruments. These family get togethers featured great home-made food (chicken and dumplings, coconut cake, banana pudding . . . you know the drill!) and always culminated with an hour or so of singing.

With Mom or me at the piano, these songfests usually began with the legends of country music (Hank Williams, Tammy Wynette, Johnny Cash) and included a little 1950s rock and roll (Elvis, Jerry Lee Lewis). Without fail, each gathering ended with hymns and Southern gospel favorites. Uncles, aunts and cousins, many while strumming guitars, lifted their voices, singing songs ranging from "I Saw the Light" to "He Touched Me." My grandmother always insisted, however, that the finale be "Amazing Grace."

The lyrics of those songs are indelibly etched in my mind. It was in these settings, and in our little country church, that I learned hymns like "Jesus Loves Me," "The Old Rugged Cross," and "Because He Lives." As a young worshipper, my theological foundation was laid around an old piano, shaping much of what I believe today.

There is little doubt Mary, the mother of Jesus, knew Psalm 121 very well. As a little girl, Mary likely sang this Psalm with her family on the five-day walk from Nazareth to celebrate the Passover. But that's not all. Because the Psalter formed the majority of worship songs for the Jewish people, the singing of Psalm 121 would've been a part of her childhood, with its words planted deep within her soul. When Gabriel appeared announcing Mary would give birth to the Messiah, she was terrified! As fear and uncertainty raged within her, the words of Psalm 121, words she sang throughout her childhood, no doubt brought her peace and allowed her to respond with her own song of praise:

> *My soul proclaims the greatness of the Lord, and my spirit has rejoiced in God my Savior, because he has looked with favor on the humble condition of his slave.*
>
> *—Luke 1:46–48*

As worshippers, we must never underestimate the power of the songs we sing. Their theological truths may be the very thing that sustains us during uncertain times.

prayer

Oh God, my fortress, thank You for being the Helper and Sustainer of those who follow You. I confess that often, like Mary, I succumb to fear and uncertainty in my life. Thank You for Your ever-constant presence that brings peace amid an ever-changing world. In Jesus' name. Amen.

What Next?

How do you face uncertainty in your life? List the things that cause you fear or panic. Next, read Psalm 121 in its entirety, listing the ways God promises to protect us through life's journey. Note how these same promises can be applied in your life and in response to the items you listed.

Day 77

Let's Go to the Church House

I rejoiced with those who said to me, "Let us go to the house of the LORD."

—*Psalm 122:1*

My first visit to Disney World was on our honeymoon in 1988 . . . but it would not be my last. Over the next three decades, with constant encouragement from three daughters who are pretty sure they are real Disney princesses, the pilgrimage to visit the "Big Eared Mouse" became an almost annual event. We love it all—the rides, the food, the fireworks. But the most amazing moment is always the same: the first glimpse of Cinderella Castle. My memories are filled with images of the girls rounding the corner onto Main Street, USA, and the awe on their faces as the castle comes into view. In that instance, it all comes to life. The movies, the music, the characters, the magic . . . everything becomes real.

Excitement and anticipation fill the days and weeks leading up to the trip to Orlando. Meal reservations are made at our favorite resort restaurants, FastPasses are secured so we don't have to spend a lot of time waiting in line, and a plan of attack is developed for each park. Nothing is left to chance.

Psalm 122 captures this same sense of excitement as the psalmist, though still in Babylon, anticipates the day when Jerusalem is restored. He longs for worship in a setting where peace and security reign. He rejoices at the thought of going to the house of the Lord.

As far back as I can remember, I've loved going to the church! Sunday was, and still is, my favorite day of the week. This shared experience with family and friends, built around worship, the study of God's Word, and relationships, builds my faith and shapes who I am. The Apostle Paul reminded us in Hebrews 10:24–26 of the importance of joining together for worship:

And let us be concerned about one another in order to promote love and good works, not staying away from our worship meetings, as some habitually do, but encouraging each other, and all the more as you see the day drawing near.

According to recent Pew Research data, only 35 percent of American Christians attend religious services regularly. Why? The answer is actually simple: people don't attend worship because they find it irrelevant to their lives. There is a lack of power, authenticity, and life change reflected in what they experience. That type of underwhelming experience can never compete with baseball and soccer games, college football, or a trip to the mall. It simply can't . . . there's not enough substance. Only a God encounter can change that.

Do you *genuinely* anticipate going to the church house? Is there a sense of awe and excitement as you walk into the place God set aside to meet with you? If not, you're missing out on one of the most important parts of your Christian walk.

prayer

Dear Lord, help me to anticipate with gladness the time when I will go to Your house. Let my visits be frequent, and let my love for You grow as I worship You. Amen.

What Next?

Take five minutes and evaluate your commitment to weekly worship.

Is church attendance a priority in your life? How does it rank when compared with your hobbies and other activities?

List three ways you can make your corporate worship this week a God event.

Day 78

Stay Focused

I lift my eyes to You, the One enthroned in heaven. Like a servant's eyes on his master's hand, like a servant girl's eyes on her mistress's hand, so our eyes are on the LORD our God until He shows us favor.

—Psalm 123:1-2

Staying focused can be a problem. How long you stay focused on a particular topic or activity is commonly known as your attention span.

A 2015 Microsoft study suggests the use of smartphones leaves humans with such a short attention span that even a goldfish can hold a thought for longer. A study of more than 2,000 participants showed the average human attention span has fallen from 12 seconds in the year 2000, or around the time the mobile revolution began, to eight seconds. Goldfish, meanwhile, are believed to have an attention span of nine seconds.

Honestly, I'm not sure if I buy the whole "goldfish-human attention span" comparison . . . although I only read the first page of the report because it was too long. I do know this: when we as Christians take our focus off God, the results are catastrophic.

The Bible is full of examples of people who lost their spiritual focus:

Adam and Eve lost focus in Eden, and sin entered the world.

Moses struck the rock instead of speaking to it and was not allowed to enter the Promised Land.

David had an affair with Bathsheba and committed murder as part of an attempted cover-up.

Jonah ran from God and ended up in the belly of a fish.

Peter denied knowing Christ in the hours leading up to Calvary.

When we take our focus off God, even for a brief moment, we are more likely to make choices that do not honor God. The psalmist understood this reality. That's why he cries out in the opening verse, "I lift my eyes to You, the One enthroned in heaven." Like a servant whose unfaltering gaze is fixed on his or her master, so should we be focused on God. This is also true in our worship. When our gaze shifts to personal preference or entertainment, our offering to God is compromised.

Resolute. Unwavering. Enduring. That's how our focus on Him should be.

In looking to Him, we find strength, confidence, commitment, and hope. When we lose focus, however, our hearts become unguarded, and spiritual failure is assured. Keep your eyes on Jesus and stay focused!

prayer

Father in heaven, thank You for Your presence in my life. Allow me to keep my focus on You in the midst of life's circumstances. Protect me from spiritual failure by binding my heart to Yours. In the name of Your Son, Jesus Christ. Amen.

What Next?

Reflect on a time when you lost your spiritual focus. What happened? Take a few minutes to make a list of things that cause you to lose focus. How can you avoid these things today?

Day 79

What If?

If the LORD had not been on our side—let Israel say—If the LORD had not been on our side when men attacked us, then they would have swallowed us alive in their burning anger against us.

—Psalm 124:1-3

I'm not a fan of "Monday morning quarterbacks." We all know them, that person who criticizes everything after the fact. I have a friend who gives the most honest and stinging post-event critiques but never offers input on the front-end. Not a great way to win friends and influence people. Because we can't change the past, the "what if" question is usually not that helpful. Psalm 124 is an exception.

One of the defining themes of the psalms is they force us to take a backward glance, a timeout, to remember how God demonstrated His power in the life of Israel. Though David doesn't identify the event, Psalm 124 was written to remember and celebrate such a victory. It reminds us God always has been faithful to keep His people in the past . . . and He will be just as faithful to sustain them in the future. He prompts them to reflect on this truth by asking, "*What if* God had not stepped into this situation?"

That's a great question for us also. Have there been times in your life when God showed up and carried you through a seemingly impossible time? While these situations may have different names (financial disaster, cancer, divorce, death), they have one thing in common: all are hopeless without God.

Psalm 124:8 leaves no doubt that God is our only reliable hope we have as His children: "Our help is in the name of Yahweh, the Maker of heaven and earth."

John Calvin, the sixteenth century reformer and pastor, used this verse as the call to worship in his church in Geneva, Switzerland, a practice that continues today in many worship traditions. A simple yet timeless truth, Psalm 124:8 establishes that God is our only reliable source of security. This truth is foundational to authentic worship.

For Christians, the ultimate source of our strength was clearly defined on a hillside outside Jerusalem more than 2,000 years ago. Because of this, Paul could declare in Romans 8:

> *No, in all these things we are more than victorious through Him who loved us. For I am persuaded that not even death or life, angels or rulers, things present or things to come, hostile powers, height or depth, or any other created thing will have the power to separate us from the love of God that is in Christ Jesus our Lord! —vv. 37–39*

Now that's a confidence we can trust!

prayer

Lord God, I am so thankful You are on my side, on the side of Your redeemed people. This is my confession: "Our help is in the name of the Lord, the Maker of heaven and earth." Amen.

What Next?

Take a few moments to reflect on a time God stepped into a situation in your life. What would have happened had He not?

Day 80

Unshakable

Those who trust in the LORD are like Mount Zion. It cannot be shaken; it remains forever. Jerusalem—the mountains surround her. And the LORD surrounds His people, both now and forever.

—Psalm 125:1-2

We live in a world gone mad. We are confronted daily with news of another school shooting, terrorist attack, or threat of war. Violence and hatred reside in our cities, and darkness seems to prevail. Murders, drugs, and rioting seems as though they are now the norm, not the exception. Political leaders spend more time fighting than leading, all while the moral fabric of the nation is unraveling before our very eyes. Against this backdrop, the future can look mighty bleak. Enter Psalm 125.

Let me confess this up front: I want to trust God. Like Mount Zion I want to be unshakable, but I often fail.

Even though I know the right Scripture passages and can vividly recall the victories God has given in my life, sometimes life leaves me, well, shaken.

I'll never forget the phone call. Immediately I knew something wasn't right. I could hear the fear in mom's voice as she explained they had found a mass in her lungs. I responded as a good, minister son should: "Hey Mom, this is going to be fine. The Lord is in control." Meanwhile, my heart was screaming from the inside, *"No!"*

For the next five years Mom lived the life of a fighter. Nonstop chemo. Radiation. Surgeries. There were many victories along the way, but as it became clear this disease would take her life, I became angry. In May 2013, Mom died. I said and did all the right things. I led worship on Sunday. I even preached her funeral. Even so, everything was not OK. We had asked God to heal her, and He didn't, at least not in this earthly life. My faith was not lost, but it was definitely shaken.

A few months later, Wendy and I were in Jerusalem celebrating our 25th anniversary. One evening as we were walking through the streets of the city, my eyes caught a glimpse of the sunset over Mount Zion. This verse immediately came to mind: "Those who trust in the LORD are like Mount Zion. It cannot be shaken; it remains forever" (Psalm 125:1).

In that moment it became clear. Like Israel, I was on a journey. After months of spiritual exile, looking back, reflecting on and even celebrating the mighty works of God in my life, my trust was restored. As Paul reminded us:

> *Death, where is your victory? Death, where is your sting? Now the sting of death is sin, and the power of sin is the law. But thanks be to God, who gives us the victory through our Lord Jesus Christ. Therefore, my dear brothers, be steadfast, immovable, always excelling in the Lord's work, knowing that your labor in the Lord is not in vain.*
>
> *—1 Corinthians 15:55–58*

prayer

Eternal One, thank You for Your ever-abiding presence in my life. In the uncertainties of life may I remember Your mighty deeds and place my hope for the future on Your victorious Son, Jesus Christ. Amen.

What Next?

Reflect on a time when something has shaken your faith. What emotions did you experience?

Memorize Psalm 125:1–2. How does truth allow us to be constant worshippers?

Day 81

From Tears to Shouts of Joy

*Those who sow in tears will reap with shouts of joy. Though
one goes along weeping, carrying the bag of seed, he will
surely come back with shouts of joy, carrying his sheaves.*
—Psalm 126:5-6

Sorrow, though an unwelcome guest, eventually visits us all,
leaving behind scars and wounds that shape who we are. How
will you respond when dealing with personal sorrow? As you
walk through hardship, will your worship become purer or will
unforgiveness silence your praise?

The life of Corrie ten Boom is an amazing story of forgiveness,
reminding us how God can turn bitter tears of sorrow into shouts of
joy. Arrested with her family by the Nazis for hiding Jews in their
Haarlem, Holland, home during the Holocaust, Corrie was imprisoned and eventually sent to the Ravensbruck concentration camp
with her beloved sister, Betsie. Betsie perished there on December
16, 1944, just twelve days before Corrie's own release. She understood what the psalmist meant when he said, "Those who sow in
tears will reap with shouts of joy."

Having stared evil in the face, Corrie could have become bitter.
She did not. In her book, *The Hiding Place*, she tells the following
story:

> *It was at a church service in Munich that I saw him, the
> former S.S. man who had stood guard at the shower room
> door in the processing center at Ravensbruck. He was the
> first of our actual jailers that I had seen since that time.
> And suddenly it was all there—the roomful of mocking
> men, the heaps of clothing, Betsie's pain-blanched face.*
>
> *He came up to me as the church was emptying, beaming
> and bowing. "How grateful I am for your message, Frau-
> lein," he said. "To think that, as you say, He has washed
> my sins away!"*

His hand was thrust out to shake mine. And I, who had preached so often to the people in Bloemendaal the need to forgive, kept my hand at my side.

Even as the angry, vengeful thoughts boiled through me, I saw the sin of them. . . . Lord Jesus, I prayed, forgive me and help me to forgive him.

I tried to smile, I struggled to raise my hand. I could not. I felt nothing, not the slightest spark of warmth or charity. And so again I breathed a silent prayer. Jesus, I cannot forgive him. Give me Your forgiveness.

As I took his hand the most incredible thing happened. From my shoulder along my arm and through my hand a current seemed to pass from me to him, while into my heart sprang a love for this stranger that almost overwhelmed me.

And so I discovered that it is not on our forgiveness any more than on our goodness that the world's healing hinges, but on His. When He tells us to love our enemies, He gives, along with the command, the love itself.

prayer

Father, I pray You will allow me to walk through times of sorrow with a hope that only comes through Your Son, Jesus Christ. Help me remember that shouts of joy await those redeemed by His blood and that joy comes in the morning. Amen.

What Next?

Take time to reflect on a Psalm 126 experience in your life. How were your tears turned into shouts of joy? What lesson from Corrie ten Boom can you apply to your life today?

Day 82

Orders Remain Unchanged

Unless the LORD *builds a house, its builders labor over it in vain; unless the* LORD *watches over a city, the watchman stays alert in vain."*

—*Psalm 127:1*

As a history buff and political science major, there's no city I would rather visit than Washington, DC. Every corner of our nation's capital presents opportunities to explore our heritage and revisit the principles, including equality, honor, liberty, and justice, that define us. Over the years, I've dragged my family through far too many Smithsonian visits, late night driving tours of the national monuments, and historic sites such as Ford's Theatre and Mount Vernon. We stood in line for the Lincoln Memorial, Ford's Theatre, and The White House, and endured the July heat to view fireworks on the National Mall. In one of our most memorable visits, in June 2004, we drove through the night in order to process through the rotunda of the US Capitol to view the lying in state of President Ronald Reagan.

There is no place more hallowed than the hills of Arlington National Cemetery. It is here where row upon row of white markers remind us of the high price of freedom. Arlington is the final resting place of many great Americans, including two US Presidents (Kennedy and Taft), several US Supreme Court justices, civil rights leaders, and war heroes. The most visited part of the cemetery, however, is the Tomb of the Unknowns, where a platoon of 30 guards protects the tomb 24 hours a day, 365 days a year, and has done so every minute of every day since 1937. No exceptions.

Each hour with the Changing of the Guard, an honor guard passes the sentinel duty to the honor guard reporting for duty in a simple but poignant ceremony. Defined by ritual and tradition, the guard from the previous hour transfers this solemn responsibility to the guard for the next hour with these words: "Post and orders, remain as directed." In other words, the orders remain unchanged—24 hours a day, 365 days a year.

The significance of worship in the life of the believer is undisputed. We were created to have an intimate and growing relationship with Him; anything short of this leaves us empty, unfilled, and powerless. The orders remain unchanged: God longs for us to commune with Him. Many times, however, our attempts at worship seem more about us manufacturing an experience than drawing to His presence. If we say the right words, create the right atmosphere, sing the right songs—then we will experience worship. The truth is, God always initiates worship; we can't create it. In a pattern of revelation and response that runs throughout Scripture, God reveals Himself to us, then we respond to that revelation.

Solomon, in Psalm 127, reminds those of us who "work" hard at worship of an important truth: unless the Lord blesses our efforts, we work in vain. His initiation is a prerequisite to worship, not an afterthought.

prayer

King of glory, thank You for creating me to be in communion with You. Forgive me for the times I try to manufacture worship and end up missing You completely. I ask that You reveal Yourself in my life and that I respond to the greatness of who You are. Amen.

What Next?

Honestly evaluate your worship life. How much time do you spend trying to "create" an encounter with God?

What are three specific ways you can improve your ability to keep watch over your heart?

Day 83

The Joy Factor

How happy is everyone who fears the LORD, who walks in His ways! You will surely eat what your hands have worked for. You will be happy, and it will go well for you.
—Psalm 128:1-2

Each week as we walk into our churches, they surround us: people who are hurting and have given up on life. If we're not careful we'll miss them, but if you look into their eyes, they cannot hide from you. Broken promises. Unexpected disappointments. Unfulfilled dreams.

There are others around us as who have experienced heartbreak, but instead of giving up, they seem to thrive in adversity. The are joyful, encouraging, and optimistic. Here's the question: what made the difference? In Psalm 128, the psalmist reminds us, "How happy is everyone who fears the LORD, who walks in His ways!" Though it seems oversimplified, it's not: those who trust in God and keep His commandments find the Lord's grace in their lives to be enough . . . no matter the circumstances.

An excellent example of this principle is William Carey, known as the father of modern missions for his missionary work in India. At a minister's meeting in 1787, Carey is said to have raised the question of whether it was the duty of all Christians to spread the gospel throughout the world. The response to him was shocking, "Young man, sit down; when God pleases to convert the heathen, he will do it without your aid and mine." Undeterred, Carey founded the Baptist Missionary Society in 1792, some five years after this happened. The following year, Carey traveled to India with his family, but his struggles continued. He saw no conversions for seven years, his son Peter died of dysentery, and his wife's mental health deteriorated rapidly. "This is indeed the valley of the shadow of death to me," Carey wrote at the time. "But I rejoice that I am here notwithstanding; and God is here."

Although he experienced much personal loss and discouragement, he translated the Bible into dozens of major Indian languages and dialects and sought social reform in India. In 1818, he founded Serampore College, a divinity school for Indians, which exists still today. At the time of his death in 1834, he had served in India for 41 years without a furlough. And while he did not see large numbers of converts, he influenced such future missionaries as Adoniram Judson, Hudson Taylor, and David Livingstone. Known for saying, "Expect great things; attempt great things," William Carey was a living example of Psalm 128.

prayer

King of the ages, thank You for calling me to be Your child. I ask that You keep my eyes focused on You when I face difficult times. May my worship be unceasing and based on Your character, not my circumstances. Give me a happy spirit as I walk in Your ways. Amen.

What Next?

Would you define yourself as having a happy spirit in the Lord? Why or why not?

How can you apply the admonition to fear the Lord and walk in His ways?

Day 84

Keep on Pedaling

Since my youth they have often attacked me—let Israel say—Since my youth they have often attacked me, but they have not prevailed against me.

—*Psalm 129:1-2*

We all could use a little *stick-to-it-iveness*. You know, that special quality that allows someone to keep on trying even though the world sees their efforts as a lost cause. These writers definitely had it:

Agatha Christie was rejected for five years before finally getting published. Now her book sales have exceeded $2 billion, surpassed only by William Shakespeare.

Dr. Seuss's first book was rejected 27 times, and he was once told that his work was "too different." Ultimately, he had 300 million sales and became the ninth best-selling fiction author of all time.

Chicken Soup for the Soul was rejected 140 times before selling 125 million copies.

C. S. Lewis's *The Chronicles of Narnia* was rejected for years before selling more than 100 million copies.

Beatrix Potter's *The Tale of Peter Rabbit* was rejected so many times that she ended up self-publishing the first 250 copies. It's now sold 45 million copies.

Perseverance pays off. Psalm 129, another Song of Ascent, calls the worshippers to remember that God will prevail against the enemy . . . we simply must remain faithful. Though still in exile, Israel celebrates the promise that God will protect her from her oppressors. When circumstances don't look great and failure is an everyday experience, the Lord's protection will carry the day.

I learned this lesson in a very tangible way several years ago. One of my friends announced he was training to participate in the Ironman triathlon. In a moment of weakness, I announced (in front of several people) if he actually finished the race, I would train and compete in a sprint-triathlon myself. To my dismay, he fulfilled his part of the deal . . . and failed to forget my part! Because my mouth had overloaded my brain, I began preparing for what would be one of the worst experiences of my life.

After several months of training, it was time to move this ill-advised idea to the "completed" column, so I registered for the race. The problem was I really wasn't physically ready. I managed the swim OK, but on the second leg, the bike, I ran into big trouble. I had assumed that riding a bike for 22 miles wasn't a big deal. I was wrong! About mile 13, 80-year olds began to pass me while encouraging me not to give up. I wanted to body slam them but felt it wouldn't be good for my ministry. Sheer pride kept me from quitting, so I finished—dead last but alive. The next day I sold my bike.

The thing about it was, no one cared that I came in last. To my friends and family I was successful. Although it wasn't pretty, I successfully finished the race and joined an elite club. I'm a triathlete . . . granted, a slow one, but a triathlete nonetheless!

prayer

Faithful God, thank You for reminding me that You're always faithful, even when things are hard. Protect me from my oppressors and keep my mind and heart focused on You. Keep me strong to finish the race. In the name of Jesus Christ, amen.

What Next?

Are there areas in your life in which you are tempted to quit? What would be the consequences of giving up? Identify one thing today you've been putting off that needs to happen . . . and do it!

Day 85

Little Boat, Little Boat

*Israel, put your hope in the LORD. For there is faithful
love with the LORD, and with Him is redemption in abundance. And He will redeem Israel from all its sins.*

—Psalm 130:7–8

Redemption, the buying back of something, is a beautiful thing. My maternal grandmother's baby brother, Z. T.
Winningham, was a Southern Baptist pastor who served
churches for more than 60 years. He was an "old-timey" preacher
man, standing six feet five, with a booming voice, and always dressed
in a suit and tie. Zach, as we called him, was called to preach as a
teenager and perfected his oratory skills in college and seminary.
Although he pastored out of state, on occasion, he would come back
home to Poplar Springs and preach a summer revival in the same
country church where he had grown up. As a young boy, I would sit
mesmerized during those weeklong meetings as Uncle Zach would
preach sermons with titles like "One More Night with the Frogs"
and "Journey through the Halls of Hell." No matter the sermon title,
redemption was the common theme.

One of my favorite stories he told was about a little boy named
Tommy who took a piece of wood and carved and shaped a little sail-
boat. Much care was taken to make sure every detail was in place.
He selected bright red paint to add some finishing touches, tied a
string to the bow, and carried it down behind his house to the creek.
Tommy carefully placed the boat in the water and slowly let out the
string. After a few minutes, he pulled the boat back to the shore,
then let it out again. For hours Tommy repeated this, in and out
. . . in and out . . . all the time admiring his toy. Suddenly a strong
current caught the little boat. Tommy tried to pull it back to shore,
but the string broke. As it rapidly floated downstream, Tommy ran
along the creek bank as fast as he could, but his boat soon slipped
out of sight. All day he looked for it. When it was too dark to look
any longer, Tommy sadly went home.

A few days later, on the way home from school, Tommy looked up and couldn't believe his eyes. Sitting in the store window was his boat. Excitedly, Tommy ran inside and yelled to the store owner: "Mister, that's my boat in your window! I made it!" "Son, I'm sorry, but someone else brought it in this morning. If you want it, you'll have to buy it for $5."

Tommy ran home, emptied his piggy bank on his bed, and counted all his money. Exactly $5! Quickly he ran back to the store and rushed to the counter. "Here's the money for my boat." With a big smile, the owner reached up, took down the little red boat, and gently handed it to Tommy. As he left the store, Tommy hugged his boat and said, "Little boat, little boat, now you're twice mine. First, I made you, and now I bought you. I'll never let you go!"

> *For there is faithful love with the LORD, and with Him is redemption in abundance.*
>
> —*Psalm 130:7*

prayer

Oh God of redemption, thank You that through the blood of Jesus I've been redeemed, paid with a price. Allow me to live a life of thanksgiving today as I reflect on the gift that has been given to me through Your Son. Amen.

What Next?

Read Romans 3:23-25 and Hebrews 9:12. Write these verses in your own words.

Day 86

Me! Me! Me!

LORD, my heart is not proud; my eyes are not haughty.
—Psalm 131:1

There's an epidemic among us. While not new and usually not terminal, every day it wreaks havoc in families, friendships, work environments, and churches. I'm talking about narcissism, which is an inflated sense of a person's own importance, a deep need for admiration, and a lack of empathy for others. Narcissism is more common than you might think, but before you strain your neck looking around to find one, you might want to pause, take a deep breath, and take a look in a mirror. One may be closer than you think.

Taken to the extremes, the traits of narcissism can blossom into a personality disorder. Although the symptoms are completely inconsistent with the character of Christ, they are far too common. A person with this disorder:

Exaggerates their own importance

Is preoccupied with fantasies of success, power, beauty, intelligence, or ideal romance

Believes he or she is special and can only be understood by other special people or institutions

Requires constant attention and admiration from others

Possesses unreasonable expectations of favorable treatment

Takes advantage of others to reach their own goals

Disregards the feelings of others, lacks empathy

Often envious of others or believes other people are envious of them

Shows arrogant behaviors and attitudes

If we're honest, each of us might have more of these traits than we care to admit. But how can a Christian, a servant of Christ, struggle with this? Truthfully, we all tend to share an inclination toward pride, insecurity, and selfishness. David knew this when he talked about pride and haughty eyes in Psalm 131:1.

In Philippians 2:5–8, the Apostle Paul told us how to avoid such traits:

Make your own attitude that of Christ Jesus, who, existing in the form of God, did not consider equality with God as something to be used for His own advantage. Instead He emptied Himself by assuming the form of a slave, taking on the likeness of men. And when He had come as a man in His external form, He humbled Himself by becoming obedient to the point of death—even to death on a cross.

When we become like Jesus, we die to self and grow in our love for those around us. Once we shift focus from ourselves to our Exalted Servant, Jesus Christ, our worship becomes a sweet sound in His ear.

prayer

Lord, I confess my inclination to be self-centered. Forgive me for my prideful spirit and attitudes that look down on others. Allow me to take on the humble character of our Lord, Jesus Christ. Amen.

What Next?

Take a few minutes and evaluate the level of arrogance and self-centeredness in your life. How are these impacting your relationships?

Take a moment and reread Psalm 131 and Philippians 2:5–8. How can you integrate the character of Christ in your life today?

Day 87

Distracted Worship

I will not enter my house or get into my bed, I will not allow my eyes to sleep or my eyelids to slumber until I find a place for the LORD, a dwelling for the Mighty One of Jacob.

—Psalm 132:3–5

TV, cell phones, emails, text messages, social media . . . technology ushered in many wonderful things, but unfortunately, it created lives without margins. There is no break from the stuff of life (work, family, friends, activities, news, etc.)—it comes home with us, vacations with us, sits on the nightstand next to our beds . . . even goes to church with us. While being constantly connected, if not careful, we will find ourselves perpetually distracted. A. W. Tozer warns of distractions in our walk with God:

Among the enemies to devotion none is so harmful as distractions. Whatever excites the curiosity, scatters the thoughts, disquiets the heart, absorbs the interests or shifts our life focus from the kingdom of God within us to the world around us—that is a distraction; and the world is full of them. Our science-based civilization has given us many benefits but it has multiplied our distractions and so taken away far more than it has given.

Psalm 132 reminds us of David's tenacious commitment to live a life of worship. Though not a perfect man, David was a man after God's own heart. His mistakes in life came when his soul became distracted, such as his affair with Bathsheba, the murder by proxy of Uriah, and the complete chaos within his family because he failed to lead them. When confronted with his failures, however, his spirit became contrite and repentant.

David, also, was committed to worship God. In Psalm 132:3–5, we see David's commitment to find a dwelling for God was so great he vowed not to sleep until he found it. In this story, told in 2 Samuel 5—6, David ushers the Ark of the Covenant into Jerusalem. He desired for God to have a permanent dwelling, a vision that would eventually be fulfilled by his son, Solomon.

For Christians, our bodies are the dwelling place of God. Like David, we must focus on preparing a dwelling for the God of the universe. In our case, this dwelling is our mind and heart:

> *Don't you yourselves know that you are God's sanctuary and that the Spirit of God lives in you?*
> —1 Corinthians 3:16

> *Don't you know that your body is a sanctuary of the Holy Spirit who is in you, whom you have from God? You are not your own, for you were bought at a price. Therefore glorify God in your body.*
> —1 Corinthians 6:19–20

prayer

Father, I ask You to eliminate the distractions in my life that keep me from You. Shine Your light on areas of my life that are negatively impacting my ability to focus on You. Protect the margins. Amen.

What Next?

Take some time to examine the margins of your life. Make a list of distractions that are impairing your worship life.

The psalmist talks about not sleeping until he finds a dwelling for God. Have you ever had that type of commitment to connect with God? What is one distraction you can eliminate today?

Day 88

Living in Harmony

How good and pleasant it is when brothers live together in harmony!

—Psalm 133:1

I live in a state that, in many ways, is defined by racial disunity. Separate bathrooms, dining rooms, and schools were simply a way of life for much of Mississippi's history. The deep emotional scars from those experiences don't heal easily.

August 28, 1955: While visiting relatives in Money, Mississippi, 14-year-old Emmett Till is kidnapped, beaten, and shot in the head. Till's murder and open casket funeral galvanized the emerging Civil Rights Movement.

March 27, 1961: Nine students from Tougaloo College are arrested for attempting to integrate the public library in nearby Jackson, Mississippi.

June 12, 1963: Medgar Evers, civil rights activist and state field secretary of the NAACP, is assassinated outside of his home in Jackson, Mississippi.

June 21, 1964: Civil rights workers are murdered near Philadelphia, Mississippi. After several weeks of searching for the missing civil rights workers, authorities found the bodies of James Chaney, an African-American Mississippi native, along with white civil rights activists Michael Schwerner and Andrew Goodman in an earthen dam.

1970: Public schools in Mississippi are desegregated. Sixteen years after Brown v. Board of Education, which ruled segregation in public education unconstitutional, Mississippi public schools are forced to integrate.

Fast-forward to June 17, 2015. After a year of rioting and violence across the country following racially charged incidents in Ferguson,

Missouri, a 21-year old demented gunman walks into Mother Emmanuel A.M.E. Church in downtown Charleston, South Carolina, and opens fire, killing nine church members. Hatred seemed to be winning . . . but worship has the power to unite and heal.

Enter the Mississippi Mass Choir (MMC), a legendary, award-winning gospel choir closely identified with my home state. Through relationships built over the years, the aftermath of the Charleston tragedy presented the perfect opportunity for a night of worship showcasing unity, not division. On August 25, 2015, more than 3,000 people, black and white, filled the sanctuary of First Jackson for Stronger Together: A Night of Unity. The First Jackson worship choir and MMC joined together to present a 500-voice expression of racial reconciliation focused on Jesus as the unifier of life. It was a sight and an experience I will never forget.

The psalmist was right when he said, "How good and pleasant it is when brothers live together in harmony!" Love, laughter, and peace define relationships forged in unity. I'll take that option over hate any day!

prayer

Father of love, thank You for allowing me to know people who are different from me. Forgive me for the times I've looked down on someone because we are different. Allow me to show love and encouragement to those around me, even if I don't understand everything about them. Amen.

What Next?

Make a list of broken or strained relationships that are hindering your worship. Repair them.

Are there people in your sphere of relationships who are unnoticed because they are different from you?

Reach out by text, email, or card to someone in your church who needs encouragement.

Day 89

Night Shift

*Now praise the LORD, all you servants of the LORD who
stand in the LORD's house at night!*

—Psalm 134:1

Y ou do what you have to do. As I began my senior year in
college, my wife of eight months spoke four words that
forever changed my life: "We're having a baby!" Although
I was excited and somewhat in shock, there was a problem. The
little country church where I served as minister of music at the time
provided health insurance, but maternity benefits required a one-
year waiting period. Since the OB-GYN required fees be paid in full
by the seventh month of pregnancy, and I didn't think the hospital
would hold our new baby girl as collateral, I took on another job
working the night shift at Hilda's Truck Stop.

Thankfully, there wasn't a lot of traffic on weeknights between 10
p.m. and 6 a.m. In fact, most of the time I could study, think, sing,
or pray (and occasionally sleep) for most of the night. And although
those were long nights, I remember how close my relationship with
the Lord grew during those early morning hours. I had some great
times of worship with just me, the Lord, and an empty store.

Sometimes the night shifts of life are more figurative—a sick child,
a broken relationship, job trouble, church conflict. In those times,
the instruction in Psalm 134:2 to "Lift up your hands in the holy
place and praise the LORD!" takes on new meaning. This became
personal when my brother Tim was diagnosed with thyroid cancer
shortly after his 18th birthday. After the initial shock of hearing the
word *cancer* as it passed the doctor's lips, we shifted into survival
mode. Surgery led to radiation, which led to trips to MD Anderson
Cancer Center in Houston, Texas, which led to other surgeries. You
know the drill. I'll never forget the grueling hours waiting for lab
results, biopsy reports, and physician updates as we hoped and

prayed for healing. Tim has been cancer-free for more than 20 years, but the memory of those night shifts is still fresh.

Several years ago I visited the tomb of Lazarus in the village of Bethany just outside of Jerusalem. As we descended the narrow, stone stairs into the belly of the tomb, I vivdly recounted every detail of the story. Days earlier, Lazarus's family sent for Jesus but he did not immediately come. Now He was there, standing outside a sealed tomb, but it was too late. Lazarus was dead. You can almost hear the frustration in Martha's voice when Jesus told them to remove the stone sealing the tomb: "Lord, he's already decaying, It's been four days" (John 11:39). As the stone was removed things began to get interesting:

> *After He had said this, He shouted with a loud voice, "Lazarus, come out!" The dead man came out bound hand and foot with linen strips and with his face wrapped in a cloth. Jesus said to them, "Loose him and let him go."*
>
> —*vv. 43–44*

When Lazarus stepped out of that tomb, Mary and Martha's night shift ended. Jesus does the same for us. Life has moments defined by fear, hopelessness, and darkness. As worshippers may we praise him in the midst of the night!

prayer

Lord, thank You for making Your presence known in the dark days of life. I confess that at times life seems to overwhelm me, but I ask that You give me courage and hope to worship through the night. Amen.

What's Next?

When was the last night shift in your life? What was the main lesson you learned through that experience? Look for someone today walking through a hard time and share the story of Lazarus.

Day 90

We Will Remember

Give thanks to the LORD, for He is good. His love is eternal.
—Psalm 136:1

Remembering where we've been is a good thing.

Over the years, I've dragged my family to more historical venues than I care to admit! Some of these journeys were fun, like the night we drove three hours just to see the Lincoln Memorial in lights or took a day trip to explore the Abraham Lincoln Presidential Library and Museum. Other times the experiences were sobering, like visiting the 9/11 Memorial Museum or Dachau, the first Nazi concentration camp opened in Germany. Regardless of the emotions invoked by each stop, the purpose of each was the same: to help us remember where we've been as individuals, a nation, and world.

Authentic worship requires we remember God's work, both in our individual lives and throughout history. Psalm 136, also known as The Great Hallel, helps us do this. Sung during the Passover meal, Jesus probably sang this psalm following His last meal with His disciples (Matthew 26:30). Written in the form of a musical timeline, the psalmist recounts God's specific work throughout history: Creation, the Exodus, the crossing of the Red Sea, and military victories as God fulfilled His covenant to Abraham. Through 26 poetic verses, the psalmist reminds us of God's work in history. He follows each verse with the same refrain to add a spiritual exclamation point: "His love is eternal."

By reflecting on where we've been, God reminds us of His faithfulness and this unwavering truth: As His love endured through past generations, it remains today . . . and continues tomorrow!

Now that's worth remembering!

For God loved the world in this way: He gave His One and Only Son, so that everyone who believes in Him will not perish but have eternal life. For God did not send His Son into the world that He might condemn the world, but that the world might be saved through Him.

—*John 3:16–17*

prayer

King of my life, thank You for the countless ways You've demonstrated Your presence to me over the years. Also, thank You for allowing us to know the history of Your specific acts through Scripture. As I reflect on where I've been and on Your presence during these journeys, I thank You for Your unfaltering and enduring love. May I reflect Your love as I live my life today. In Jesus' name. Amen.

What Next?

List three ways God worked in your life during:

The past week

The past month

The past year

The past ten years

As you reflect on God's work in your life, reread Psalm 136, focusing on His work in the history of the Israelites. When we stop to remember what God has done for us, our natural response is to worship Him.

Day 91

Have You Lost Your Song?

By the rivers of Babylon—there we sat down and wept when we remembered Zion. There we hung up our lyres on the poplar trees, for our captors there asked us for songs, and our tormentors, for rejoicing: "Sing us one of the songs of Zion." How can we sing the LORD's song on foreign soil?

—Psalm 137:1–4

The past year had been hard for Dave. He had major challenges with his business. His kids were now grown, married, and live far away. Aging parents and unrelenting financial issues raised his stress to a whole new level. These challenges, combined with a period of intense church conflict, left Dave shaken . . . in spiritual exile . . . seemingly alone and isolated.

Dave was no marginal Christian. He loved the Lord deeply, taught Sunday School, sang in our worship ministry, and served in the leadership of our church. Even so, life had taken its toll. Sitting in my office, Dave looked me squarely in the eyes and spoke some of the saddest words I've ever heard, "Lavon," he said, "I've lost my song."

Psalm 137 finds Israel in a similar predicament. Having been conquered by Babylon, Israel finds itself in a foreign land. The psalmist paints a dark, vivid picture—in exile, filled with bitter tears and haunted by memories of Zion, their harps are now silent. Their voices were silent.

Exile has that effect. Nothing makes sense. Our foundations are shaken. Hope seems distant.

Like the psalmist, our hearts cry out, "How can we sing the LORD's song on foreign soil?" The truth is, for a season, you probably can't. Too much pain . . . loss . . . anger. Although it's hard to believe, a day will come when you will sing again. It may be slow and painful, but eventually the notes will return. You'll take the harp off the willow and sing again!

For the Christian, our ability to sing again comes from our relationship in Jesus Christ. We worship the Lamb of God who has overcome sin, death, and the grave. We worship the Creator of the universe who holds this world in the palm of His hands. We worship the Eternal God of heaven who has no beginning or end. The Great I Am. And one day we will join in singing: "Worthy is the Lamb that was slain to receive power, and riches, and wisdom, and strength, and honour, and glory, and blessing. . . . Be unto him that sitteth upon the throne, and unto the Lamb for ever and ever!" (Revelation 5:12-13 KJV).

prayer

Lord, I confess at times I allow my mind's attention and heart's affection to veer away from You. Give me the grace I need for this season of exile. I ask You, Lord, to restore my joy and let me sing again. I pray in the name of Jesus. Amen.

What Next?

What song is your heart singing today? Is there even a song at all, or have you hung up your harp?

Write down five blessings in your life. How should these define the song of your heart?

Day 92

Strength Rising

On the day I called, You answered me; You increased strength within me.

—Psalm 138:3

Have you ever been in a deep, dark place? From my experience, if you haven't been there yet, one day you will be. The kicker is—will you be prepared for it when it hits you?

David had lots of experience with deep, dark places. He seems to handle them one of two ways: (1) he replaces his focus of what God wants with what he wants (that whole episode with Bathsheba comes immediately to mind), or (2) he does what he professes in this verse—he calls on God (prays), God answers (we do not know if God answered as David may have specifically asked but we know He did answer), and God gave David strength to face it. Knowing myself well, I can say with certainty I am also like this.

David prayed for relief from Saul and got it. I expect he prayed before confronting Goliath. He certainly would have made better decisions had he prayed before he sinned with Bathsheba and then having Uriah killed. We need to look closely at the differences in outcomes. And we need to think about how this applies in our own lives.

In Luke 22:42, we hear Jesus' prayer: "Father, if You are willing, take this cup away from Me—nevertheless, not My will, but Yours, be done." A nonbeliever might wonder (and in fact, sometimes believers wonder!) how God could turn His back and not answer His Son's prayer. I believe God did answer that prayer. I believe God did exactly as David said in the latter part of Psalm 138:3—God made Jesus bold and strengthened His soul. I personally believe God could have saved Jesus from that Cross. I also believe Jesus could have saved Himself. But neither of these things happened. Jesus died a death more awful than anything I can imagine, and He did that so I could live always—eternally—with Him. My sins were totally covered in His blood. And in order to accomplish this,

I believe that a strength that could only come from God was placed in Jesus' soul. And that, to me, is amazing love.

In Psalm 138:8, David says: "The LORD will fulfill His purpose for me." When Jesus came, died, and rose again—the Lord accomplished without question what concerns me. For this, I am eternally grateful.

prayer

Father, I thank You for giving Jesus everything He needed to die for me. Lord, I praise Your name and ask now that You give me everything I need to share this news boldly with those around me. Amen.

What Next?

Think about prayers that the Lord answered, whether immediately or over time, and how He answered them. How did God strengthen your soul?

Day 93

Imago Dei

I will praise You because I have been remarkably and wonderfully made. Your works are wonderful, and I know this very well.

—Psalm 139:14

I look a lot like my mom. In fact, it's been said I'm her "spittin' image." Not only do we share many physical attributes, we have similar personalities, dispositions, and mannerisms. Mom died in 2013 at the age of 61 from lung cancer. Not a day passes that I don't think about her and feel grateful for the many things she passed down to me.

Mom loved music . . . so do I.

Mom had big eyes that telegraphed her thoughts . . . so do I.

Mom loved to tell stories . . . so do I.

Mom loved to laugh and make others do the same . . . so do I.

Mom loved her family unconditionally . . . so do I.

Mom had this amazing ability to make each person feel as though they were the most important person in the world . . . I'm still working on that one!

Psalm 139:14 reminds us that we are remarkably and wonderfully made. Genesis 1:27 takes this to a whole new level when it says we are created in the *imago Dei*: the image of God. Just as parents pass along traits to their children, God desires us to resemble Him. The more time we spend with Him, the more we begin to look like Him. The more we worship God, the more we take on His image. When that happens, the fruit of the spirit become a reality in our lives: love, joy, peace, patience, kindness, goodness, faith, gentleness, and self-control (Galatians 5:22-23). I don't know about you, but I'll take those traits any day!

prayer

Loving Father, thank You for creating me in Your image! I confess that I fail every day in living out Your holy attributes, but today I ask that You give me opportunities to display them to people around me. Allow me to love unconditionally, demonstrate joy in all circumstances, speak peace in conflict, show patience when rattled, display kindness to everyone, pursue goodness in all my actions, live out faith in a world filled with doubt, radiate gentleness in all my deeds, and model self-control, no matter what happens. Amen.

What Next?

You reflect the image of someone. Decide now if you will be the image of the One who created, loved, and sent His Son to die for you or not. His traits are worth pursuing and will make all the difference in your life and the lives of those around you. Who will you look like today?

Day 94

Taming the Tongue

LORD, set up a guard for my mouth; keep watch at the door of my lips.

—Psalm 141:3

Words are powerful. They can bless and encourage. They can also assassinate a person's character and create a sense of negativity that can overshadow someone's life. Like an archer releasing an arrow, once launched, words cannot be recalled.

Afterward, we may struggle with our thoughts. *I wish I hadn't said that. I'm sorry.* But usually the damage is done—hurt feelings and damaged relationships. Forced into full-scale cleanup mode, lifting words of praise to the King of kings and Lord of lords can be derailed. An untamed tongue kills our ability to worship.

Several years ago, I worked through an exercise that underscored the importance of words. On a sheet of paper, I listed the five most significant compliments received in my life. Reflecting on this list, I was reminded how various people had used words to encourage and edify my life. These included a fourth-grade teacher who encouraged a stuttering young boy to speak in front of the class and a college professor who encouraged me to write.

I then shifted to the dark side and listed the five most hurtful criticisms of my life. Even years later the impact of the negative words stung. The raw emotions uncovered by these lists reinforced the truth referenced in Psalm 141:3: words matter.

Words hurtfully spoken are not a mouth problem; rather, they are a heart issue. Jesus points this out in Luke 6:45 when He says, "His mouth speaks from the overflow of the heart." Our words are one reason why the spiritual condition of our heart is so critical.

So how do you use your tongue?

Are you using your words to encourage or tear down?

In the end the words we speak are a spiritual choice. How are you using yours?

prayer

Lord, thank You for the power of words in my life. Forgive me when my own words have been used to tear others down or spread negativity. I ask that today You tame my tongue, allowing it to be instrument of Your peace. In the name of Jesus. Amen.

What next?

List the five most meaningful compliments of your life.

List the five most hurtful criticisms of your life.

Identify someone to bless this week with your words . . . and do it!

Day 95
Trapped

Listen to my cry, for I am very weak. Rescue me from those who pursue me, for they are too strong for me. Free me from prison so that I can praise Your name. The righteous will gather around me because You deal generously with me.

—*Psalm 142:6-7*

As a guy who suffers from claustrophobia, exploring caves (also known as spelunking) is not at the top of my bucket list. Not so with Floyd Collins. On January 30, 1925, while trying to find a new entrance to Crystal Cave in central Kentucky, Collins became stuck in a narrow crawlspace 55 feet below ground. Pinned in place by a 27-pound rock, Collins couldn't move. The ensuing rescue operation prompted what was possibly the first media frenzy in American history, with national newspapers and broadcast radio setting up shop to cover the rescue effort. For four days, rescuers brought water and food to Collins. That ended when a rock collapse closed the entranceway to the cave, trapping him for two weeks with only voice contact. Floyd Collins was alone.

While everyone experiences loneliness at some point in their lives, we live in a time some researchers have coined the "Age of Loneliness." This designation is based on estimates that one in five Americans suffers from persistent loneliness resulting in health issues such as heart disease and depression.

David understood loneliness. In Psalm 142, he fled Saul and hid in a cave. This man after God's own heart was isolated from family and friends and, in a real sense, trapped by life's circumstances. Many of us may find ourselves in a similar position: discouraged, hopeless, lonely, even depressed. How should we respond?

David gives us a great example. In the midst of despair and uncertainty, he worships: "I cry to You, LORD; I say, 'You are my shelter, my portion in the land of the living'" (v. 5). There will be times as Christians when we find ourselves physically, mentally, or spiritually alone. In these times we must confidently rely on God as our refuge, our place of safety and security.

We can survive only so long in isolation. After being trapped for 14 days, Floyd Collins died inside Crystal Cave of thirst, hunger, and hypothermia. Similarly, spiritual isolation damages our relationship with God to the point that our worship is rendered powerless and ineffective. Left trapped, we experience a slow but certain spiritual death.

prayer

Dear Lord, I confess that I am lonely. I ask that You show me ways to connect with others so I can be removed from isolation. I commit to rely on Your strength to help me overcome the spiritual cave in which I reside. Amen.

What Next?

Read 1 Samuel 22:1-9. Reflect on a time you were in spiritual isolation. What are three key lessons you learned?

$\mathcal{D}ay$ 96

Anger Management

The LORD is gracious and compassionate, slow to anger and great in faithful love.

—Psalm 145:8

We all know folks with a short fuse. Nearly anything can set them off. Frankly, in most cases, it becomes an annoyance dealing with them. Unfortunately, they can also be dangerous because their explosions tend to injure people in their paths. Relationships are destroyed due to hurt or annoyance. Mostly it is just tragic.

Then, there are the slow-burning fuses—I have a friend like that. He is so subdued that sometimes you want to check his pulse! He's easy going, is a friend to many, and one of those guys who does not like or want the spotlight but does a lot of ministry in the background. Things like repairing faulty wiring, filing taxes for folks who can't afford to hire someone, building sets and staging for First Baptist Jackson's Christmas production Carols by Candlelight, or meeting financial needs—all without any fanfare or the recipients knowledge of the beneficiary. But—when his fuse blows—it is major. Interestingly, the catalyst of his blowup is always someone's continual incompetence. Fortunately, he does not personally attack when in that state, but you can rest assured if he was doing business with you, he is done with you.

This verse in Psalm 145, also appears in similar form elsewhere in the New Testament:

Then the LORD passed in front of him and proclaimed: Yahweh—Yahweh is a compassionate and gracious God, slow to anger and rich in faithful love and truth.

—Exodus 34:6

Tear your hearts, not just your clothes, and return to the LORD your God. For He is gracious and compassionate, slow to anger, rich in faithful love, and He relents from sending disaster.

—Joel 2:13

God has every right to be angry with us, but His compassion often spares us from that. Yet there are times for righteous anger. Jon Bloom says, "Righteous anger is being angry at what makes God angry. And 'righteous anger' is the right word order. Because God is not fundamentally angry. He is fundamentally righteous. God's anger is a byproduct of his righteousness." Because God is perfectly righteous, His anger comes slowly and after much warning.

Bloom goes on to say, "If you want to see love-governed anger in operation, look at Jesus." Most often when I think of Jesus' anger, I think of when He cleared the Temple of money changers (Matthew 21:12). People coming to the Temple needed sacrifices. These could be obtained at the Temple. Unfortunately, the religious leaders at the time had turned people's needs for sacrificial animals into a for-profit racket. Jesus was having none of it. His anger was righteous. God sent Jesus for a purpose, and during Jesus' time on earth He was subjected to many things that angered God. Jesus could have battled in a traditional way, but He did not. He used Scripture and in this specific case acted out against this abuse occurring within God's house. He did this out of love for His Father. Just as He died out of love for us.

prayer

Lord, I confess that my anger is seldom righteous. Forgive me for anger directed against others. Help me to be more like Jesus—to act and react in love for others out of my love for You.

What Next?

Find other references to God's anger. Record these in your journal and the circumstances surrounding the verses. What do you see?

Day 97

Back to the Future

Our Lord is great, vast in power; His understanding is infinite.

—*Psalm 147:5*

Many of us have seen, probably multiple times, the 1985 movie *Back to the Future*. If you like comedy and sci-fi, it is a classic combination. It is probably Michael J. Fox at his best. Seriously, a DeLorean capable of time-travel! The very thought of that is funny.

Psalm 147:5 comes at the end of a passage about the past and the future. This chapter is one of the five Hallelujah Psalms that close the Book of Psalms. Each one opens with "Praise the Lord!" literally "Hallelujah!"

Psalm 147 was likely written to celebrate the return of the Jews to Jerusalem from Babylon. Though in the presence of a king, the prophet Nehemiah mourned over his people's exile and the destruction of Jerusalem. When King Artaxerxes asked Nehemiah why he was sad, Nehemiah prayed and made a request, "If it pleases the king, and if your servant has found favor with you, send me to Judah and to the city where my ancestors are buried, so that I may rebuild it" (Nehemiah 2:5). And over the course of some 55 days, Nehemiah did rebuild the wall and the Jews returned to Jerusalem from exile in Babylon. As the psalmist states in Psalm 147:2–3, "The LORD rebuilds Jerusalem; He gathers Israel's exiled people. He heals the brokenhearted and binds up their wounds."

The psalmist also gives us hope in the future in verse 4: "He counts the number of the stars; He gives names to all of them." In other words, God cares. He has all the wisdom and talent required to count something apparently as infinite as the stars in heaven and to give them names. If He can do all that (as well as take care of lilies in the fields as we are told in the New Testament), why do we ever doubt the future and His care for us?

We are often like the church at Laodicea in Revelation 3:15–17: "I know your works, that you are neither cold nor hot. I wish that you were cold or hot. So, because you are lukewarm, and neither hot nor cold, I am going to vomit you out of My mouth. Because you say, 'I'm rich; I have become wealthy and need nothing,' and you don't know that you are wretched, pitiful, poor, blind, and naked." We are lukewarm in our faith, a condition that causes us to look past what we really are—sinners in need of a Savior!

As we learn from the past and look to the future, let's do it with faith, knowing that God remains true to His promises for those who acknowledge Him.

prayer

Lord, I confess my faith is often lukewarm and that I rely on myself and not on You. Lord, I choose to trust You—You loved me enough to save me. Help me to be bold like Nehemiah, seeking Your will and then being persistent in following where it leads. Amen.

What Next?

Read the Book of Nehemiah and study how God uses Nehemiah's obedience to return the Jews from exile.

What sort of exile are you in? Do you trust God to bring you out of it?

Is your future secure? Have you chosen Jesus or are you chancing your future?

Day 98

Praise the Lord!

Let them praise the name of Yahweh, for His name alone
is exalted. His majesty covers heaven and earth.
—*Psalm 148:13*

This song is all about praise. One of the Hallelujah Psalms, there is no question this psalmist was filled with thanksgiving and was bold in telling all aspects of creation that they needed to be praising God too.

The hymn that immediately comes to mind is "All Creatures of Our God and King." St. Francis of Assisi wrote the words back in 1225. William H. Draper, an English clergyman, translated it into English around the year 1910. This hymn is based almost entirely on Psalm 148. If you study the words of the six stanzas against the words of Psalm 148, it is easy to see the inspiration.

Of greater interest to me is that many believe Frances was nearly blind when writing it, so he wrote from his life experiences. A wealthy young man at birth, he chose a life of poverty and service as a friar and died destitute. "Canticle of the Sun," the prayer upon which "All Creatures of our God and King" is based, is a reminder of our need to praise God without failing, for all His creation, from the glory of the Sun to the remarkable nature of the smallest insect.

My favorite verse is the final stanza of the hymn:

Let all things their Creator bless,
And worship him in humbleness,
Alleluia, alleluia!
Praise, praise the Father, praise the Son,
And praise the Spirit, Three in One:
O praise him, O praise him,
Alleluia, alleluia, alleluia!

Oh, to see Creation through the eyes of the Creator! How much greater and humbler would our worship be?

prayer

Lord, I praise You. I want to praise You in every possible way. I know even more I should be humbled by Your presence all around me. Thank You for never leaving me or forsaking me. Amen.

What Next?

Read Psalm 148 in its entirety and contrast it with the creation story of Genesis 1-2. Does the psalmist leave out anything in his admonishment to us to praise the Lord?

Day 99

Sing A New Song

Hallelujah! Sing to the LORD a new song, His praise in the assembly of the godly.

—Psalm 149:1

Today's various worship cultures often find us balancing sides between singing the old hymns, many of them the same way as we always have, and singing songs that some of the people in the room don't know, don't like, and don't believe have anything much to do with worship. Honestly, both camps need to take a step back and look at their reactions. First, Jesus was all about change. Second, you must tell the old, old story to get to Jesus, and that can be done in a variety of ways.

In 2007, our worship choir and some of our band members spent a little more than a week in Saint Petersburg, Russia. It was eye opening. Even for those who had traveled internationally, several even to Russia, we saw things from a perspective we could not have imagined.

The resident missionary cautioned us that when attending church at Central Baptist Church in Saint Petersburg, a partner church to First Jackson, we would be in a zone we would not recognize. While we were allowed to sing, our production used drums (oh my!), an instrument that had only been used maybe one time in that building previously. Afterword we sat, trying to stay upright on the hard choir loft seats, while two very long sermons were shared in Russian. When church ended, we felt as though we had escaped. No one smiled. Very few sang. Reactions were almost nil. And we were going back that night to do a full concert.

Sure enough, we come back. Our missionary reminded us again to keep a lid on any exuberance in our worship. The crowd was much the same—many babushkas (Russian grandmothers), very few men (most of those the age of the grandmothers likely died in WWII), a good smattering of young adults, and some small children. But the church was full. I remember thinking this was going to be a long night. But, as God is prone to do, He showed up and showed out. We were singing "Days of Elijah"—a favorite of ours. Songwriter Robin Marks said: "The song is generally and principally a song of 'hope.' . . . I felt in my spirit that He replied to my prayer by saying that indeed He was very much in control and that the days we were living in were special times when He would require Christians to be filled with integrity and to stand up for Him just like Elijah did, particularly with the prophets of Baal." Since we had been cautioned, we were subdued, but God had another plan.

This new song sparked something. You could feel the electricity in the room. Looking up in the balcony, a young woman stood, raised her hands in the air, and worshipped. It took off like wildfire. Soon every child, adult, and babushka was literally dancing before the Lord! I had not experienced anything like that before and have not since. They were hungry for worship, hungry to share their love for Jesus, and hungry to hear more. We sang everything we knew and a good part of it twice. We stood in the courtyard of that wonderful church loving on them and them on us after we finished. They heard many new songs that night. Why that one opened their hearts, I will never know. But even in our reticence and desire not to offend them, God had control and opened the doors to their hearts.

prayer

Lord, open the eyes of my heart. Encourage me to sing a new song of praise to You every day. Thank You for the shared experience of worship. Help me to be hungry for more. Amen.

What Next?

Think about a time the Lord placed a new song in your heart. What was your reaction to it?

Day 100

The King of Glory Has Arrived

Hallelujah! Praise God in His sanctuary. Praise Him in
His mighty heavens. Praise Him for His powerful acts . . .
Let everything that breathes praise the LORD. Hallelujah!
— Psalm 150:1–6

In January 1985, I had the privilege of attending the inaugural celebration for President Ronald Reagan. The intense cold notwithstanding (they canceled the inaugural parade because of freezing temperatures), the entire experience was defined by grandeur, majesty, and a sense of excitement that permeated the entirety of Washington DC. Patriotic banners were hung from buildings, US flags were displayed on every street, and thousands of people filled the city to celebrate the beginning of a new presidential term.

A highlight of the week was the Inaugural Ball at the Kennedy Center. As people mingled and danced, an excitement began to build as the crowds anticipated the arrival of the Reagans. Eventually it happened. The United States Marine Band played the traditional trumpet fanfare, after which a voice announced, "Ladies and gentlemen, the President of the United States." As President and Mrs. Reagan stepped onto the stage, the musical strains of "Hail to the Chief" filled the room, confetti and balloons were dropped from the ceiling, people were applauding . . . the President had arrived!

Unfortunately, our worship seldom rises to this standard. As we reflect on the greatness of God and respond to His mighty acts in our lives, the psalmist directs "everything that breathes" to praise Him with instruments of all kinds—trumpets, harps, tambourines, flutes, stringed instruments, and cymbals. In Psalm 150 we are encouraged to give everything we have as we lift our praise to the God of the Universe.

As exciting as a presidential inauguration can be, it pales in comparison to standing in the presence of *Yahweh Nissi*, the Lord is our banner. When we see Him in the fullness of who He is and what He's done, everything about our worship will change. The psalmist says, "Let everything that breathes praise the LORD!" The question is, will you do your part? Ladies and gentlemen, the King of glory has arrived!

prayer

Oh God of heaven and earth, this morning I lift my praise to You simply because You're worthy. As I reflect on who You are and the ways You've worked in my life, I offer my unfiltered praise. Your greatness surrounds me, and today I pray my heart will be a symphony of worship to You as I live my life. Amen.

What Next?

Reflect on the different ways God's greatness is visible around you this morning. Next, list ways you can tangibly offer your worship to God with a Psalm 150 "all in" attitude. Your day will be blessed because of it!

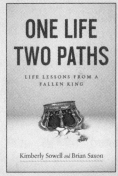

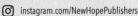

New Hope® Publishers is a division of WMU®, an international organization that challenges Christian believers to understand and be radically involved in God's mission. For more information about WMU, go to wmu.com. More information about New Hope books may be found at NewHopePublishers.com. New Hope books may be purchased at your local bookstore.

Please go to NewHopePublishers.com for more helpful information about *Tuning Your Heart to Worship*.

If you've been blessed by this book, we would like to hear your story. The publisher and author welcome your comments and suggestions at: NewHopeReader@wmu.org.